A Sentimental Economy

New Directions in Anthropology
General Editor: Jacqueline Waldren

A SENTIMENTAL ECONOMY

Commodity and Community in Rural Ireland

Carles Salazar

Berghahn Books
Providence • Oxford

First published in 1996 by
Berghahn Books

Editorial offices:
165 Taber Avenue, Providence, RI 02906, USA
Bush House, Merewood Avenue, Oxford, OX3 8EF, UK

Library of Congress Cataloging-in-Publication Data
Salazar, Carles.
  A sentimental economy : commodity and community in rural Ireland /
Carles Salazar.
      p.   cm. – (New directions in anthropology : v. 2)
  Includes bibliographical references and index.
  ISBN 1-57181-887-1 (alk. paper)
      1. Ireland–Rural conditions. 2. Ireland–Economic Conditions–
1949–.   I. Title. II. Series.
HN400.3.A8S25 1996
307.1'412'09417–dc20   96-33871
                                                                        CIP

British Library Cataloguing in Publication Data
A catalogue record for this book is available from
the British Library.

Printed in the United States on acid-free paper.

They are a wild and inhospitable people. They live on beasts and live like beasts ... For given only to leisure, and devoted only to laziness, they think that the greatest pleasure is not to work, and the greatest wealth is to enjoy liberty. This people is, then, a barbarous people, literally barbarous. Judged according to modern ideas, they are uncultivated, not only in the external appearance of their dress, but also in their flowing hair and beards. All their habits are the habits of barbarians. Since conventions are formed from living together in society, and since they are so removed in these distant parts from the ordinary world of men, as if they were in another world altogether ...

– Giraldus Cambrensis
Topography of Ireland, 12th century

CONTENTS

Contents

PREFACE

The serious contradictions embedded in capitalist civilisation became widely apparent in the nineteenth century. Among these were the tensions between equality and fraternity, community and association, status and contract, mechanical and organic solidarity, capital and labour. Max Weber realised that one of the contradictions is that as capitalist society becomes more economically 'rational', in terms of means-to-ends relations, at the same time it becomes more culturally 'irrational' in terms of the ends it pursues. Likewise the tension between economic rationality and social cohesion and between economic rationality and religious meaning was a central theme of his work. Behind much of this was the attempt to keep spheres apart, in particular to separate the social from the economic.

These contradictions are particularly ripe for analysis now because of three strong tides. The first is that 'capitalism' is spreading rapidly all over the world. The one major attempt (apart from Islam) to hold together spheres, to stop alienation, to prevent the social, economic, political and ideological spheres from breaking apart – namely the totalitarian approach of Utopian communism – has disintegrated. Hence we need to analyse the currently 'winning' system with particular care.

Secondly, the very rapid penetration of 'market forces' is destroying the major alternative social system which blended the economic and social spheres over most of the world until very recently. As late as 1950 over three-quarters of the peoples on earth were 'peasants' who based their economic system on the domestic mode of production. The 'European peasantry' was largely destroyed between 1950 and 1990. The other half of the world, in Asia, comprises over two billion 'peasants' who are rapidly becoming petty capitalists, totally subject to 'market forces' and replacing family with other forms of labour.

Thirdly, it is clear that the central activity of humans in both 'peasant' and 'capitalist' societies is changing very rapidly. It is an irony that as Marxism as a solution is abandoned, many of Marx's prophecies are being fulfilled in a slightly different form. Marx foresaw that as 'capital' increased, the 'workers' would be dispensed with, becoming an under-class or reserve army. The situation is much graver than this, for almost *everyone* is now surplus to requirements. We now see that as technology (condensed knowledge and capital) makes both the muscles and brains of humans largely redundant, 'work' can no longer be the central activity of humans.

Most societies in the past have determined their existence in terms of status, that is, fixed position in terms of birth. Yet with the development of a particular brand of Christian (Calvinist) capitalism in the West, work became the key to both economic and moral value. For the majority of the population a new situation developed in which there is very little else by which either rewards (money) can be obtained or people can judge their worth, other than by work. 'I work therefore I am.' This historical situation creates a crisis. The one objective standard in the double sense of financial and moral value is now crumbling as we move to a world where very little human work is needed. What happens when the whole set of moral, social and economic laws which were based on the premise of the widespread necessity and availability of work is no longer valid?

A number of these huge changes and problems focus our attention on the precise interface between the social (family/'status') and the economic (economy/'contract'). The Japanese deal with some of these contradictions by blending the two elements into what has been termed 'kintract' *(Hsu)*, or what we might call 'artificial status'. That is, they operate precisely a 'sentimental economy', mixing the warmth of 'community' with the efficiency of 'association'. Historically they did this through their unusual family system, that is to say, through flexible adoption. Somehow they have transferred this into the modern 'family-like' firm. How are the growing contradictions dealt with in the West?

One way in which to approach these important problems is to focus on the central issue, namely, work. This is what Dr. Salazar does. The second is to concentrate precisely on that activity which has for various reasons tried to entangle the economic and the social, namely, farming. The attempt to separate economy and society causes a particular problem in the case of small farming, because historically (and for intrinsic reasons, because of the diffuse, open-ended nature of farming), farming in many places has represented the last bastion of the domestic mode of production (DMP). Indeed the DMP is precisely that fusing of family and economy. How does such a system operate as the power of the market increases?

One solution to the problem of understanding complexity, as Durkheim realised, was to analyse an 'elementary' case. This is what Dr. Salazar does. He makes it possible to go deep into the problem by delimiting the area of observation, by 'seeing a world in a grain of sand' in the time-honoured anthropological way. He takes just sixty-five households in County Galway in the west of Ireland. He largely ignores much of their world, for instance, politics and much of religion. He concentrates on their work practices – what they do, how they do it, and with whom they do it – and what they think they are doing.

His insights are of interest for several reasons. He puts his findings within a framework of wider theory. He uses a true comparative model, that is to say, one where he can compare another case (Catalonia, where he has done parallel fieldwork) to see similarities and differences. He has used the participant method of anthropology in the best way, by becoming deeply immersed in the tangle of people's lives and by working side by side with them in the fields. He has penetrated below the surface of their lives in an unusual way, perhaps helped by the fact that he is both outsider (Spanish) and insider (European/at an English university/Catholic). He has seen this world as both familiar and strange, a tension caught in the excellent photographs.

He is thus able to explore the contradiction that lies behind much of life in capitalist economies and which is caught in his title, *A Sentimental Economy*. He explores the way in which humans construct their world so that the deadening hand of market transactions and the greying effect of money and bureaucratisation of work are muffled, reinterpreted and socially reconstructed so that they do not make life intolerable

Dr. Salazar shows how the harsh realities of market capitalism are masked by the representations people have. What appear as balanced reciprocities to the outsider are seen as generalised, unbalanced, noncalculating. The trick is to maximise economic efficiency and to make life socially meaningful. By behaving in one way, and thinking one behaves in another, the contradiction can be partly overcome. This becomes manifest in the chapter on ritual. God needs to be efficiently manipulated, put under pressure to 'deliver the goods'. On the other hand, God ought also to be treated in a noninstrumental and general way and not expected to respond automatically to human pressure.

Thus Dr. Salazar illuminates some profound areas lying on the borderline between economy and society. This book is a subtle, sympathetic and well-written account. It adds, I believe, a valuable case study to the distinguished set of works that have been produced on the 'Irish Countryman'.

King's College, Cambridge   Alan Macfarlane

ACKNOWLEDGEMENTS

*F*rom the economic point of view, this research was possible thanks to a doctoral scholarship from the Ministry of Education and Science of the Spanish government. From the intellectual, moral and emotional viewpoint, my greatest debt of thanks is owed to Alan Macfarlane, who supervised the initial version submitted as a Ph.D. thesis at the University of Cambridge in 1993. I am also grateful to Rosemary Harris and Frances Pine for their useful and supportive suggestions during the oral examination. There are also many friends and colleagues who have contributed to the realisation of this project. Chris Curtin gave me invaluable help while I was 'in the field'; technical assistance was lavishly offered to me by the staff of the Agricultural and Food Development Authority (*Teagasc*) of Athenry, in the Republic of Ireland; Ray Abrahams, Nick Barker, Jesús Contreras, Heonik Kwon, Josep R. Llobera and Ignasi Terradas read and commented on earlier drafts; I obtained a priceless friendship and affection from Carmen Avalos and Montserrat Guibernau during the arduous process of writing; André Czeglédy-Nagy and Alison Field helped me to polish my English; Domi Mora and Xavier Ribas took care of the editing of my photographs. Last but not least, I dedicate this book to the people of the west of Ireland, whose names cannot be mentioned here but without whom nothing of what follows could ever have been written.

INTRODUCTION

Ever since the very early research conducted by Arensberg and Kimball in the 1930s, surely one of the first anthropological studies of a European society, Ireland has been considered as a sort of cultural oddity in western Europe. From different perspectives and at different levels, and maybe together with the Mediterranean regions, it has been seen as a contemporary and west European example of a form of society that otherwise could be studied only through historical records or in Third World countries. The pervasive power of familism (Arensberg and Kimball 1937, [1940], 1968), the preservation of archaic kinship structures (Fox 1978), the omnipresence of religious institutions (Inglis 1987) and religious and ethnic factionalism (Harris 1972), not to mention cultural fossilisation and exoticism (Messenger 1969, Scheper-Hughes 1979), political clientelism (Bax 1970), a bizarre demographic pattern (Kennedy 1973), and colonialism and economic underdevelopment (Brody 1973) are all classic themes in the analysis of 'premodern' or 'peasant' cultures that soon found their way into Irish ethnography. It would not be easy to work out a common thread that could draw together such a varied set of narratives, but still we should remark on two closely interconnected subjects that appear to be particularly recurrent (see Wilson 1984).

Possibly because these issues were also major interests of Arensberg and Kimball, students of Irish rural society seem to have been predominantly concerned with the significance of kinship and family structures in relation to a specific type of domestic organisation known as the stem family model and, on the other hand, with the intricate question of the rationality of such a model as regards the small farmers' economy. I will refer to these issues later on in more detail. Important methodological questions have also been brought to the fore: the suitability of the traditional anthropological tool of analysis, intensive participant observation, when dealing with a complex society, and the associated problem of generalisation out of a singular monographic study – as it happens, relevant questions as well in Arensberg and Kimball's work.

To make explicit one's options in response to the scientific context in which a particular research claims to participate is always a tricky endeavour. But it is certainly useful to delineate at least some interpretative clues. Concerning the methodological question, my line of enquiry is clearly defined by the type of qualitative analysis derived from the method of participant observation, carried out in a farming community of the west of Ireland. Even though, to avoid repetitions, I will indiscriminately use expressions such as 'the west of Ireland', 'rural Ireland', 'Irish farmers' and the like, there are no claims to any general applicability of my findings beyond the group of families I worked with. As for the more substantive question, it is the economy as a social construct and as a cultural experience of a community of small farmers that defines the object of my research, and comes to show, incidentally, the intimate link that binds the object to the method of analysis. It is, therefore, from this methodological perspective, and its parallel substantive implications, that the economic relations of the farming community will be understood within the framework not only of particular forms of family organisation, but also in the wider context of their 'extra-economic' environment.

My strategy to understand the social life of family farmers was suggested by the very practice of ethnographic research. Doing fieldwork in the west of Ireland one soon realises that no matter what may be the anthropologist's purpose or the particular aim of his or her research, as soon as he[1] starts to assimilate into the people's culture – by this I basically mean as soon as he starts to be able to participate in people's day-to-day conversations in a matter-of-fact manner – he will find himself talking about farming and about farm work in any of its different manifestations (ecological, economic, psychological, emotive, etc.) sometimes almost against his own will! It is as if the discourse about farm work constituted a sort of elementary social language, a basic system of communication by means of which much of the social interaction of the community could develop, and the knowledge of which was almost

---

1. The masculine pronoun will generally be used in this book to refer to abstract subjects.

indispensable for any stranger trying to become a temporary member of that community.

'Labour connected with agriculture', Arensberg and Kimball wrote, 'is merely one feature of a total constellation of behaviour enforced through obligations reciprocal in nature and maintained by sentiments and sanctions in a traditional setting' ([1940] 1968: 78). This is a culturalist-institutionalist manifesto that has legitimated the scepticism of more materialist and individually oriented scholars (Harris 1988: 423). In a similar vein, an American folklorist has written that work gives to the small farmers of Co. Fermanagh 'the thickest, most serious way to form and test their thought' because if we consider them 'as tellers of myths and as naturalists, twice we will come to the same conclusion. Work is a way to think' (Glassie 1982: 577, 579). But what does farm work have that makes it suitable for such an unusual application? What sentiments and sanctions turn agricultural labour into a feature of a total constellation of social behaviour? The following pages will illustrate how farm work obtains this strange capacity to defeat any narrow economic definition.

I first went to the west of Ireland with the vague idea of looking at cooperative institutions among small farmers. But after some introductory interviews, I began to think that those institutions had disappeared long ago from the Irish countryside, and so there did not seem to be many possibilities of carrying out my research proposal. To make things worse, I had not been able to find accommodation in a family farm, as was my initial intention; although the family I was staying with was closely related to the farming community, it seemed to me that I was not getting the whole picture of the social world, whatever it was, of the farming families of that community. Soon I realised, however, that there were two ways of entering into a family farm. One of them was, certainly, living there, but there was also another one: working, because working in a family farm is also a way of *living* there. And this is how my participant observation started to take shape. Offering my help to the farmers of the community is how I managed to break into their hermetic houses and, from there, into the secluded privacy of their social lives. And so I could redefine the objective of my research in the following way: as an exploration of the social universe of a community of western Irish farmers that tries to answer a 'simple' question: how is work socially construed in a family farm? Thus, farm work turned out to be the object of my analysis by being also my method of research.

After the first six months of intensive/informal participant observation, I was working more or less on a regular basis for three different farmers; even though I had already been able to document their respective social networks, I decided that it was time to collect information in a more systematic fashion. Some data needed quantification: average land ownership, family size, etc. I needed a census of the community and also some sort of sociological sample. But then I had to solve first an apparently trivial problem: where exactly was 'my community'? Thus far I had been gathering qualitative information without paying too much attention to the existence of administrative or other types of boundaries, which seemed to me irrelevant for my purpose. Family farms in the west of Ireland are not gathered in villages but scattered all around, either on their own or in small hamlets of four or five houses. But since all my key informants happened to belong to the same parish on the one hand, and on the other, I had already made some use of the parochial institution – announcing my arrival in the parish newsletter, finding accommodation through the parish priest – I thought that the parish boundaries were the only ones that, in a certainly loose way, could define the spatial limits of my research.

In this sense, the fieldwork on which this book is based took place within the parochial boundaries of a little church in the northeastern part of Co. Galway, approximately ten miles from Galway city. The parish includes roughly three District Electoral Divisions, so I will call it from now on the Three Districts. According to the census of 1986 (the only one available at the time of my fieldwork) the Three Districts have a population of 1,400 inhabitants distributed in 353 households, of which 178 are recorded as farm households, 50.42 percent, including 748 inhabitants, 53.43 percent. It was from here that I took a random sample of 65 family farms, 36.52 percent of all the family farms of the Three Districts, with whom I cross-checked through in-depth interviews the qualitative data obtained through participant observation *strictu sensu*. Less systematic information was also gathered from 33 more families, which together with the other 65 adds up to 98, 55.06 percent of all the family farms of the area.

The average land holding of my sample is 56.9 acres, slightly larger than that of Co. Galway, 48.1, which in turn is also a bit bigger than the 46.1 acres corresponding to the west region (counties of Galway, Mayo, Clare and Roscommon) (Ó Cinneide and Cawley 1983: 29). I deliberately excluded from my research marginal farms with little or no economic significance for their owners. I was interested only in people for whom the farm constituted the basic source of income. Soon it became clear, however, that a sample of just full-time farmers exclusively dependent on the profits they could reap from their farm business would have been totally unrepresentative of the farming community of the west of Ireland. In fact, only 23 of my 65 family farms claimed to have no other source of income than the farm and, making allowances for a certain tendency to understate off-farm earnings, I suspect that there were probably even fewer. Thirteen out of the other 42 were part-time farmers, and the remaining 29 combined different sources of income such as Small Farmers' Assistance, pensions, working wives, etc. More detailed information about this sample will be provided in later chapters.

I have said that the economy as a social construct and a cultural experience constitutes the object of this research. But in fact, for reasons that will become clear later on, the economy constitutes only the starting point; the object of analysis can only reveal itself as the description develops. Let us have a quick look at the structure of this description.

The book could be divided in four parts. In the first three chapters, I have tried to articulate three different perspectives on the fieldwork stage. The anthropologist's perspective is in Chapter 1, a certain sense of the 'native's point of view' is in Chapter 2, and the perspective from the discourse of political economy in Chapter 3.

The following four chapters present a description of the economic life of western Irish farmers. My understanding of this economic life is based on a constant dialogue between two theoretically antagonistic principles. On the one hand, there is the principle of commodity exchanges, not only as the connection of the farm economy with the rest of capitalist society (Chapter 4) but also, and more importantly, as a principle that designates a particular type of social relationships: those based upon the notion of contractualism. A contractual relation can be defined as that which takes place between anonymous subjects involving the exchange of determinate services and counter-services. This is just another way of talking about the exchange of commodities.

Chapters 5, 6 and 7 deal with different manifestations of the contractual principle as they apply to the organisation of farm work in the Three Districts. But as we deepen our analysis of the farming economy, the ideal type of contractual relation becomes more and more twisted by the unruly penetration of 'extra-economic' interferences. Formal contracts give way to tacit transactions, commodities become gifts, the economic turns itself into the social. The theoretical antithesis of the commodity form acquires an increasing prominence, until it places itself at the very centre of the analysis. We see in Chapters 8 and 9 how the economy is beginning to dissolve into wider fields of social interaction.

The dissection of these fields of social interaction is the objective of Chapters 10, 11 and 12. Finally, in Chapter 13 there is an attempt at some sort of theoretical synthesis and an open-ended, quasi-experimental, proposal in Chapter 14.

What follows can be seen as a prolonged transition from the abstract to the concrete, from the economic to the social, from the universal to the local, from theory to representation. This is a smooth transition devoid of any sharp discontinuity. It is rather full of ambiguous spaces, wherein subjects and objects lose one definition and gain another. There is neither a pure community ethos nor a pure market rationality, but a complex and untidy combination of both – perhaps because there are no totally isolated cultures in rural Ireland, but rather they all partake, in their specific ways, in universal systems of meaning – an ambiguous situation that explains much of the particular profile of my research.

My fieldwork in the west of Ireland lasted from April 1990 until June 1991, after which I spent two further months in a farming community of central Catalonia (in the northeastern part of Spain) with the idea of gaining some form of distance from the 'total immersion' in the Irish countryside, and trying to gather at the same time some preliminary data for future comparative research. A full account of this second fieldwork cannot be included here, but references will be provided whenever I think it worthwhile for a better understanding of my Irish material.

1. MEMORIES FROM THE WEST

As Bourdieu has emphasised, we can no longer advocate the scientific status of anthropology without knowledge of the conditions of anthropological knowledge. Participant observation, he writes, 'is, in a sense, a contradiction in terms (as anyone who has tried to do it will have confirmed in practice) … The participationist option is simply another way of avoiding the question of the real relationship of the observer to the observed and its critical consequences for scientific practice' (Bourdieu 1990: 34). What follows can be taken as an attempt to come to terms with this inherent contradiction of participant observation. It is an attempt to bring to the fore precisely the real relationship between observer and observed, not so much as a claim to 'authenticity' of anthropological knowledge, but as one of its constituent parts.

Let us begin with a quick glimpse at the fieldwork stage. The *dramatis personae* of this story are middle-sized farmers from a western Irish community. The farmers of the Three Districts belong entirely to what we could call the rural culture of the west. 'This is the west of Ireland', 'here in the west of Ireland' were the standard expressions people would use to identify themselves when talking to me. Yet we should make it very clear that this research is not about the small crofters of the western shore, who seem to have attracted the majority of anthropologists interested in rural Ireland.

The stereotyped version of what a western Irish landscape looks like, the version that we can easily gather from dozens of tourist brochures, does not really reflect an accurate image of the Three Districts. Fields are much bigger than the small gardens so emblematic of Connemara cottages, for instance, and agricultural machinery is rapidly replacing the romantic images of donkey-carts. A conspicuous lack of mountains and picturesque sceneries, on the other hand, whilst it allows the development of modern farming technology and, therefore, the subsistence of a more dynamic farming community, has kept the local universe relatively safe from the alienating effects of tourist culture. A somewhat paradoxical result.

I pointed out in the Introduction that the area of the Three Districts corresponds loosely to the parochial boundaries of one of the local churches. It includes one main village, surrounded by a handful of farmhouses and small hamlets of four or five dwellings.[1] The structure of the village is very simple: it has only one street, with a wide green space in the middle which was an old cricket field of the British landlords, people told me. There are also a Garda (police) station, a post office, a couple of shops, four pubs and the remains of an old Protestant chapel. People say that long ago there was also a Catholic church, but it was burnt down by the landlord of the moment. He was very fond of impregnating young peasant girls, so the story goes, until the Catholic priest decided to denounce him at Mass, and then he took his revenge against the church building. From then the Catholic Masses have been said in a little chapel half a mile away from the last village houses.

There is no description of the Three Districts that I can think of clear enough to provide the reader with an idea of what my fieldwork scene looked like. As a matter of fact, the Three Districts as some form of objective entity do not exist; they are very much the effect of my particular relationship with the community. They were created in a lengthy and painstaking process of interaction, understanding and representation of the local culture. In this process, different spaces succeeded each other in changing my perception as I was making progress in my ethnographic practice. These were the public spaces of the church and the pub, the domestic sphere of the private house and the intermediate domain of the

---

1. Village settlement does not have much tradition in Ireland because of the monastic, rather than diocesan, organisation of the Celtic Church. Furthermore, the works of the Land Commission in the late nineteenth and early twentieth centuries, while trying to join the old scattered patches of land into compact holdings, also contributed to the dispersal of the rural population (Freeman 1969: 134). Evans argues, on the other hand, that in Ireland people do not need to agglomerate near water sources, for instance, because water is not a scarce resource (1942: 47–48); this is apart from the fact that in a pastoral economy a village settlement is clearly inappropriate, since the farmer needs to be near the stock most of the time (1957: 23).

farm. There is nothing specific in the definition of any of these spaces but my personal introduction into each of them. In the case of the church and the pub, the resulting relationship did not go beyond an initiatory and rather superficial approach. Concerning the house and the farm, in contrast, the interaction turned out to be deeper and more productive.

The church certainly constitutes one of the epicentres of the community. I must say that the friendliness of the local priest provided me with a kind of moral infrastructure for much of my research. It did not seem to me, however, that there was a great deal of intimacy between the parish priest and his parishioners. Despite, or maybe because of, the considerable moral authority that a parish priest still holds in rural Ireland, his relationships with the local population have a strong taste of the coolness and social distance of a hierarchical bond. As far as my research was concerned, this meant that my relationship with the parish priest could not be taken as the scaffold for the building of an effective social network. I had to look elsewhere for the possibility of closer contacts. So my first direct interaction with the 'natives' did not take place through the church but in one of the local pubs.

But once again, the suitability of this type of interaction as a springboard for deeper relationships appeared to be more than questionable. Very little of my fieldwork was actually done in those idiosyncratic meeting points of the west of Ireland. Soon I realised that very little 'serious' information could be gathered from the sort of hopelessly informal conversations that I could mix in or start off in a pub. Furthermore, my initial lack of fluency in the local dialect discouraged me from entering into too many or too jocular relationships with the locals, which is the customary type of interaction that you would find in an Irish rural pub. 'Group conversations in Ballybran are, indeed, laden with double-talk, obfuscations, interruptions, and non-sequiturs, which make it difficult for the uninitiated outsider to follow and participate … Verbal ambiguity is a common response of a defeated people towards their conquerors – that is, never giving the master a straight answer' (Scheper-Hughes 1979: 82). Whatever may be the reasons for this oral murkiness, I was glad to hear that native English speakers had similar problems.

The disappointing results of my work in both church and pubs made me shift my attention directly to private houses. If the public spaces turned out to be so shallow, it was a matter then of jumping straight into the domestic domain. Certainly, individual interviews in private houses proved to be more productive at these early stages of my fieldwork. There was nothing of the joking mood of the pub, I happily realised, and so the dialogue could be kept at a more accessible level for the uninitiated outsider. But, alas, after the first four or five interviews of this sort, it became clear to me that neither could this be a conclusive *way in*. I was falling into, if I may use this expression, the 'sociologist trap'. First of all, the type of information that could be obtained was somehow already encapsulated in my own questionnaire. I would learn nothing really new. I could not think of that procedure as a genuine ethnographic practice.

On the other hand, an interview provides a very biased image of social life. It is biased by the very interaction of the interview itself: a dramatic reproduction of the subject/object dichotomy that is very far from the sort of humanistic ethnography I wished to carry out. Moreover, and quite obviously, it is only conscious information that can be elicited from an interview and, worse than that, it is information belonging to the sphere of 'discursive consciousness' (Giddens 1984: 7). The majority of social relationships go well beyond the restricted range of the subjects' verbal competence. The necessity of a deeper or more immediate form of interaction became the nightmare of my first 'initiation' nights.

The house and also the farm, as we will see later, could not be turned into significant spaces for my cognitive practice without the mediation of an explicit and consistent social relationship – much more explicit and consistent than had been the case with the public spaces of church and pub. If ethnography appears not only as a way of looking at the world but also, first and foremost, as a way of being in the world, one can never content oneself by observing social life in a more or less participative mood. The practice of ethnography is no less a *creative* activity than the writing of it. We can observe social relationships only by creating social relationships. All this appeared to me with crystal clarity as I attempted now and again to break into the impenetrable privacy of the house.

A radical change in the conditions of my ethnographic knowledge came with the meeting of my host family, a definitive turning point in my fieldwork experience. This certainly provided me the intellectual satisfaction of being able, at long last, to observe people 'from within'. No less importantly, it gave me the indispensable emotional support to overcome the most depressing and frustrating periods of my fieldwork. The relationship with my host family turned out to be excellent right from the beginning. There was an undeniable economic incentive in the actual possibility of our interaction: I had to pay a monthly rent for my room. But it soon became clear that our contractual arrangement was becoming increasingly overshadowed by the powerful extra-contractual bonds that we were able to build upon it. These were bonds substantiated by all sorts of material transactions, such as lifts to town, baby-sitting services, any kind of domestic help and by transactions with a much stronger emotional content, such as the exchange of presents on special occasions and, more particularly, the happy crystallisation of a long-lasting friendship.

'We wouldn't like you to stay in your room all the time, we would like you to mix with us', my hostess informed me the very first day of our meeting. It will be apparent from the following chapters that this gradual, but never definitive, abrogation of an economic link by the powerful imprint of extra-economic bonds, which so well defines the relationship with my host family, constitutes a pervasive topic of this research. It might be because in the case of ethnography, the objective conditions of knowledge always include the subject of the cognitive process. This does not necessarily defile the objectivity claims of such a process, provided that we become explicitly aware of its personal component.

As was mentioned in the Introduction, no matter how deeply and productively the interaction with my host family happened to develop, it turned out to be insufficient in the long run. This can be explained by the family-centred structure of the community. With the exception of farming families – and this is an important exception, as far as my argument is concerned – social life in rural Ireland develops mainly within private houses. And even for farmers, their extrafamily relationships appear strongly biased toward their family universe, meaning that no close contacts can be expected from any public space. But it also means that deep interaction with a single family does not lead by itself to knowledge of the rest of the community;[2] above all if this single family happens to be a non-farming family – as was the case with my host family. More particularly, on the other hand, for several reasons that are not relevant to the present discussion, my host family did not appear to have a very extensive social network within the locality.

I decided then that somehow I had to build that social network myself, and so I started to look for work on the farms of the community.

---

2. 'To be at home with the Irish countryman as his friend for any reasonable length of time is to come to know virtually every family in the rural community. This is due to the essential structure of that community and an enlightening clue to its nature. For in rural Ireland the farm family is typically small, yet in nearly every rural community the small farm family is the centre of power' (Humphreys 1966: 11). There does not seem to be much evidence to support this assertion as far as my fieldwork experience is concerned and, precisely, because of the same reasons that Humphreys puts forward to elaborate his argument. The family-centredness of the community inhibits, rather than helps, the extension of the interaction of one family with any other.

Once the space of the house had become accessible thanks to the relationship with my host family, the next objective was similarly to defeat the inaccessibility of the farm. Thus the second social relationship began and my ethnographic practice started to take shape.

I never worked for pay, since I made it clear right from the beginning that my intention was to do research and not to make a living. Setting aside the question as to whether this would agree with fieldwork ethics, the existence of a monetary transaction between myself and my 'employers' could have blocked, or seriously impaired, so I thought, the development of the other type of transaction that I was especially interested in, the transaction of information. Putting it another way, to become a full-time farm worker would have meant the abrogation of observation by means of an unacceptably close participation. 'The critique of objectivism and its inability to apprehend practice as such in no way implies the rehabilitation of immersion in practice' (Bourdieu 1990: 34). Furthermore, the imbalance between what I could obtain from the men I was working with in terms of data for my research and what I could offer to them in terms of a bit of help on their farms was so vast, that it seemed to me utterly outrageous if on top of that I asked for money. By rights it should have been the other way around!

On the other hand, the lack of an economic transaction in this case conferred upon me an ambiguous role, particularly in the first weeks. It was difficult for them to understand what I was up to, killing myself on their farms for no pay. At the same time, they did not have much trouble in getting rid of me in a, perhaps cynically, respectful way. They thought that I was doing it just 'to please them' and, therefore, their corresponding moral obligation was to prevent me from being too lavish in my generous behaviour, that is to say, to prevent me from working as much as possible – just the opposite of my wishes. As it is practically impossible to treat an Irishman to a drink, since he will always insist on footing the bill even to the extreme of creating an argument, it is no easier to offer him any assistance that he might perceive as purely disinterested aid.

A relation of generalised reciprocity is always predicated upon a bond of trust between parties. My refusal to accept any pay for my work turned the relationship with the farmers into a generalised reciprocity exchange with very indefinite counter-services. I was creating a debt with them that they did not know how to repay, nor even whether they would be able or willing to repay. In other words, I was trying to create a relation of generalised reciprocity without any preexisting bond of trust. The crucial importance of this requisite became very clear to me just after the first week of working for one of the local farmers.

This had been the first house I came across while doing my first interviews. The friendly welcome they provided me encouraged me to ask the farmer whether I could come along to do a bit of work for him from time to time. Everything went all right until one morning he told me that he could not employ me on his farm any more: 'You have no insurance, you see, if anything happened to you the courts would be very sympathetic to you and I could lose a good bit of money.' 'You can come for a cup of tea whenever you please,' he added, 'but you'd better keep away from the farm.' No matter how many different ways I put it to him that I would never raise any legal claim against him, it was to no avail. The truth of the matter was simply that he did not trust me.

It was in this way, therefore, through my own ethnographic practice and, especially, through the mistakes of my own ethnographic practice, that I came to know the nature of a very important social relationship in the community. In later chapters we will have the opportunity to go deeply into it.

Thus, the combination of these two types of social relations – with my host family and with the farmers I worked with – constituted the conditions of my anthropological knowledge. One appeared as a contractual agreement containing all sorts of extracontractual ingredients that decisively distorted its formal character. The other consisted of a relationship of informal aid that could develop only by means of the gradual formation of a bond of trust. To some extent it could be argued that it was my effort to understand and come to terms with my own role within the community, as a putative family member and as a no less putative farm worker, that accounts for much of what follows.

We have seen in this chapter an ethnographic snapshot 'from the anthropologist's point of view'. We have seen the Three Districts first as a simple piece of landscape, a visual evocation. Then it has become the stage of different types of social relationships that gradually enabled the metamorphosis of that visual perception into the object of a cognitive practice. In the following chapter we are going to shift our perspective. Let us imagine that we can perceive the local community through an image that is no longer the anthropologist's image.

2. Languages and Practices

*N*othing could be more simple for the people of the Three Districts than the aim of my research when I told them that I wanted to know about their work. Their work has to do above all with the care of their animals. 'He who lives among Nuer', Evans-Pritchard wrote in a much quoted ethnography, 'and wishes to understand their social life must first master a vocabulary referring to cattle and to the life of the herds' (1940: 19). We could similarly argue that the language of cattle and sheep plays a comparable role among western Irish farmers even if not as pervasively as among the Nuer, to the extent that the specific weight of animal husbandry as such for sedentary pastoralism has been considerably reduced to the advantage of land husbandry. The culture of animals constitutes in fact just the tip of the iceberg of a much more complex set of cultural constructs and social activities, all of them, however, stamped by the demands of their final aim: the production of livestock. Therefore, there is also a 'bovine idiom' to be learnt if one wishes to understand the social life of western Irish farmers.

The purpose of this chapter is to make the reader familiar with the language of work among western Irish farmers, as I have already pointed out its importance in the configuration of the social interaction of this community. The animal husbandry culture of western Irish farmers is not a verbal culture, rather it stems from their everyday practice working with their animals and it is validated by the effectiveness of that practice, not by explicit articulation of its principles.[1] Therefore, it is

1. 'People know what they are doing. Their actions prove it. They dibble sets in the moss of ridges and have food for the winter. They give their surplus to their

precisely to this everyday practice we must turn if we are to make any sense at all of their idiosyncratic jargon.

Let us have a quick look at the general features of animal husbandry in the west of Ireland. Pastoralism is a ubiquitous characteristic of Irish agrarian history. In fact, only exceptional historical circumstances, such as the need to supply the British markets before the repeal of the Corn Laws, or later, the Emergency period during the Second World War, made it profitable for Irish farmers to grow anything other than fodder for their animals. Official statistics tell us that cattle raising constitutes nowadays the main farm business in the western counties: 66.3 percent of all livestock units, followed by sheep, 16.9 percent, and dairy cows, 14.6 percent – the remaining 2.2 percent are classified as draught animals (Ó Cinneide and Cawley 1983: 20). In my sample of 65 family farms, 14 have only cattle, 3 only sheep, 47 combine cattle and sheep and 1 has only dairy cows. Out of those 65, 12 add a few dairy cows to their dry stock, 18 keep some sort of draught animals (horses, ponies, donkeys, etc.), and 2 rear a few pigs. The combination of cattle and sheep appears thus as the most common enterprise. Nowadays, except for draught animals, practically all the livestock raised in western Irish farms is produced as a commodity.

According to the National Farm Survey for 1989, farms specialised in cattle had the lowest average incomes, only 30 percent of the overall average, while mainly sheep systems had about two-thirds and dairy farms, by contrast, yielded roughly double that average (National Farm Survey 1989: 4). Given the high income of dairy farms, the preference for cattle and sheep enterprises does not seem to make any sense. Should not dairy farming instead of dry stock be the most widespread farm business? Several reasons might account for this apparently groundless choice. The system of quotas established by the EEC from 1983 onward prevents anyone who at that time did not have dairy cows from getting into the dairy business, unless he can buy a quota from a dairy farmer. On the other hand, the lack of piped water in the area of the Three Districts decisively hampered the development of dairy farms on a major scale at the time the quotas were set up. Furthermore, dairy is much more work-demanding than dry stock, hence totally unadvisable for

---

neighbors and have help in time of need. They speak grammatically and repress harmful ideas and live peacefully among other creatures. What they cannot do easily is translate rightness into a language distinct from normal action. They display knowledge by acting correctly rather than by describing action' (Glassie 1982: 642–43).

part-time farmers, and even for mixed farmers who want to combine it with other farm enterprises.

Neither does sheep specialisation seem a feasible alternative. Although sheep farms are more profitable than cattle farms, they require a bigger acreage and, again, the work demands of sheep husbandry are far bigger than those of cattle husbandry, especially with a good few heads. The easily flooded meadows of the low plains of Co. Galway add another disadvantage to sheep raising, since sheep cannot thrive in wintertime if their wool is constantly soaked with water.

These facts explain why mixed farms of cattle and sheep predominate in the western region, despite the low profits they yield in comparison with other farm systems. When farmers are asked why they have cattle and sheep, they invariably respond that 'you should not put all your eggs in the same basket'. Many different diseases may spread throughout a herd, but will not affect animals from different species, so that a risk-minimising strategy is clearly suggested by such combination of two types of livestock (see Leeuwis 1989: 48–49). And we should not forget, on the other hand, that direct subsidies represent more than 40 percent of the income on cattle farms and more than a half on mainly sheep systems, while they account for very little of the incomes of dairy and other types of farms (National Farm Survey 1989: 4).

The cultural ecology of pastoral farming demonstrates many characteristics of agricultural economies in general terms. It is assumed that the dependence of this type of economy on natural cycles determines quite rigidly the parallel cycles of their productive processes. In the case of Irish pastoral farming, the ecological cycle is divided into two seasons, summer and winter, according to the way the animals are fed. During the summer season, usually from April until November (depending on the weather), livestock graze freely in the fields; during the winter, due to the impossibility of moving the herd to fresh pastures as would be the case in a nomadic or transhumant society, stock have to be fed with fodder. This opposition winter/summer represents the cornerstone of the ecological culture of Irish farmers, and it provides the integrative rationale of all the labour processes constitutive of the farming process of production.[2]

Foddering, cleaning, dosing, dipping, milking and the general care of livestock, particularly intensive during the lambing and calving seasons,

---

2. All farming communities have in common their dependence on the weather and natural cycles for the implementation of their processes of production, but this dependence manifests itself in many different ways. To take just another interesting

constitute the farmers' main occupations with regard to their animals. They are dirty and tiresome jobs that have been unequally affected by the mechanisation of farm labour processes. There is no fixed social form for their implementation; they can be carried out individually (foddering, cleaning, milking), with the help of neighbours or family members (dosing, dipping) or under some form of contractual agreement (cleaning, dipping). But the culture of animals and animal husbandry, as was noted at the beginning of this chapter, is just the tip of the iceberg of the much larger set of social activities, constituting what we could call the cultural system of pastoral farming in the west of Ireland. This extension of that cultural system beyond the sphere of animal husbandry has been brought about by the sedentary nature of western Irish pastoralism.

The important point to stress is that sedentarism for a pastoral society enlarges the sphere of its work practices into the realm of the care of the land. For a sedentary pastoral society, therefore, the landscape is not just the physical location of the rights of way, as is the case for their nomadic cousins, but the physical location of their rights of work. It follows from this that, together with the 'bovine idiom' there is also a 'land idiom' to be understood.

We can approach the land idiom of western Irish farmers by looking at the four categories in terms of which they classify their landscape: bog, tilled land, meadows and rough pastures. The allocation of land within these four divisions has to be related to the characters of the soil and climate. But perhaps with the exception of the bog, those types of landscape do not invariably stem from the austere imperatives of nature; far from this, most land will alternately become crop land, meadow and rough grazing according to the necessities of its human dwellers. Even bog can be reclaimed and turned into pasture or arable land.

Those four categories of landscape can be associated, on the other hand, with different aspects of Irish history and culture. We will see that the work at the bog constitutes one of the pillars of a stubbornly 'self-sufficient' domestic production. Crop land seems to evoke likewise the hated times of the landlords' economy, recalling both its subsistence and commercial-surplus-extractive side in the cultivation of potatoes and

---

example, Catalan stockbreeders of the plains also depend on the weather for such important things as the growing of their crops, but this dependence gives rise only to a mere seasonal allocation of some tasks, and by no means to the radical split between the winter world and the summer world that I have observed among Irish farmers (cf. the English 'factory farming' described by Newby 1979: 75–119).

corn, respectively. Grassland hints clearly at pastoralism, that all-pervasive element of Irish agrarian history we have just been examining. The meadows, finally, qualify that pastoralism with the additional feature of sedentarism, the type of pastoral farming prevailing in Ireland at present.

Whatever might be evoked by this classification of the landscape, it manifestly results from a perception of the land as an object of work, and it is from this specific consideration that all value that land might possess – economic, political, emotive or symbolic value – should be assessed. Let me begin then with the first domain of our classification.

The bog is a 'wet, spongy, poorly-drained ground consisting largely of decaying vegetation', according to the definition of an ordinary English dictionary. Wide, brown surfaces of bog land constitute one of the most remarkable characteristics of the Irish scenery. The bog is where farmers obtain turf,[3] indispensable fuel for domestic use in the majority of rural dwellings practically since the late seventeenth century, when after the forest clearances that took place at that time the native population had to look for an alternative to timber (Evans 1957: 182–83). Access to bog land is regulated through a complex combination of different types of rights. Turbary rights entitle their holder to cut turf from a particular plot; the right of ownership entitles its holder to regain the full property of the plot over which somebody else has turbary rights once the turf has been exhausted. Apart from these, the owner of turbary rights can 'sell a plot of turf', which means that a third party can buy the turf already cut and save it himself. Out of my sample of 65 farm families, only 15 do not cut their own turf, most of them because their original plots have been exhausted. Five of these 15 buy plots of turf, 4 buy the turf already cut and saved, one cuts the turf in his brother-in-law's bog, and the remaining 5 use oil or other types of fuel. None of the 45 families who cut their own turf sell their produce.

The turf harvest usually begins by mid April, and it is the first task of the agrarian cycle in the west of Ireland. Except for the odd one who still likes to do things manually, the process of turf cutting is nowadays fully mechanised. A contractor comes along with two bulky machines and in a few minutes fills the whole surface with a coat of soggy sods. Mechanisation, however, has not reached the process of saving the turf. Once the sods have been cut, they are not ready for use until they are dry, and

---

3. 'Turf' is the word used in Ireland to refer to what in Britain is commonly called 'peat'.

this is the purpose of saving, which involves turning each sod upside-down one by one, building stacks and eventually bringing it all to the shed – a back-breaking work for which the more people that can be recruited the better.

Let us now leave the bog and move to a very different type of land-scape. As we go westward in the Irish countryside it becomes increasingly difficult to come across any patch of tilled land. It could not be otherwise if we take into account that the wet and cold climate of the western regions makes them quite unsuitable for any type of crop, especially corn. Statistics conclude that only 10 percent of the total agricultural land of the Irish state is devoted to crop growing (Sheehy and O'Connor 1985: 27). In the western counties (Galway, Clare, Mayo and Roscommon) this is further reduced to 2.5 percent, which amounts to 7.3 percent of all land suitable or moderately suitable for tillage (Ó Cinnéide and Cawley 1983: 9 and 16). Tillage farms, on the other hand, seem to be quite lucrative for their owners; they yield the highest average income, together with dairy farms (National Farm Survey 1989: 14), although they only account for 6 percent of all Irish farms. The problem with tillage is that it requires a good bit of land to make it profitable, twice as much as a dairy farm to obtain similar returns (Commins 1990: 10), which is why tillage is so rare among the small farmers of the west of Ireland, especially as a commodity production.

The potato is perhaps the most suitable crop for western Irish ecological conditions. Introduced in Ireland by the mid-seventeenth century, it would certainly be an exaggeration to say that the history and culture of the Irish countryside can be summarised in a social biography of the potato, but there is no doubt that its prominent role cannot be easily questioned. In my sample of 65 farm families I came across 30 potato growers. Only 8 of those 30 mentioned the sale of some surplus to local shops or potato merchants; the rest produce mainly for themselves, although the majority of farmers remembered having grown potatoes at some stage in years gone by, even on a commercial basis. But if it is true that only a few farmers produce potatoes nowadays, it is no less true that all of them consume potatoes on a regular basis. Not a single dinner did I eat without that indispensable ingredient. So much so that in the month of July, when the previous harvest has been already used up and the new potatoes are not ready yet, more than once I had to accommodate myself to just one salad for the day because my landlady could not even think of preparing a dinner without a few spuds. It is no wonder that the month of July was traditionally known in Ireland as the 'hungry month'.

Potatoes are sown between April and May, and the harvest takes place from September onward, although early potatoes can already be collected in August. Mechanisation has greatly simplified the labour processes involved both in preparing the land and in planting the crop, but for the final picking a significant amount of manual work is still required.

We will meet some potato pickers in a later chapter, but now let us turn our attention to the culture of corn, the other important crop grown in the Three Districts. I have already remarked on the adverse ecological context that the west of Ireland provides for this type of agricultural production. In such an unfriendly climate, oats certainly appear as the more suitable grain. Apart from their use as animal fodder (horses and sheep), oats have also constituted since time immemorial a habitual element in the human diet, being the basic ingredient for oatmeal. Barley, on the other hand, never seemed to endure the Irish wet weather. Its common application was for brewing beer, ale and porter, and in the distillation of whiskey and poteen (homemade whiskey) (Bell and Watson 1986: 179–80). Only lately has it started to be used as animal fodder. Apart from the grain, straw from both oats and barley has traditionally had several applications: both types of straw come in handy for livestock bedding, barley straw may substitute for hay in times of scarcity, and oat straw is still used for thatching roofs.

There are 37 corn growers among the 65 farm families of my sample. Thirteen out of those 37 claim to sell some surplus, either to merchants, to the creamery cooperative or to neighbours. As we saw in the case of the potatoes, the majority of those who do not have any corn at the moment also confirmed that they grew it in the past, first as surplus producers, later only for self-sufficient purposes and eventually they gave it up altogether. Another similarity to the potatoes is the fact that, whether they produce it themselves or obtain it from someone else, all farmers need corn, but in this case they need it for foddering purposes, that is to say, for productive consumption – an important difference from the case of the potatoes.

Corn is sown in springtime, from early April onward (Good Friday was the customary day to begin sowing), and the harvest takes place around September (the Irish word for September, *fomhar*, means literally 'harvest'). Once again, mechanisation has substantially altered the labour processes involved in corn growing. Sowing is done with a self-propelled seeder provided by a contractor, and the old and laborious tasks of reaping, binding, stooking, stacking, flailing and winnowing, greatly simplified with the introduction of threshing machines, are now carried out by combine harvesters, also provided by contractors. It is interesting to note that both literary and oral sources agree in underscoring the effervescence of the collective work that the use of threshing machines brought about.[4] There is a curious paradox in the transformations of the social context associated with the introduction of threshers. As Bell and Watson have pointed out, 'a lot of writings dealing with "modernisation" tend to assume that changing techniques mean less mutual help', whereas in this particular case, the 'use of co-operative working relationships between neighbours provides one of the clearest examples of technological' change actually strengthening these links' (1986: 217). But threshing machines have now been fully replaced by the modern combine harvesters, which do the whole job of harvesting, leaving the corn almost ready for consumption. We will see later on to what extent that atmosphere of sociability activated by the old threshers can still be felt with the latest technological innovations.

Apart from corn, the other important crop grown in the Three Districts until very recently was sugar beet. But the closing down of the Tuam sugar factory in 1986 made its cultivation practically disappear among the local farmers. There is only one big grower in the Three Districts now, and he sells all his produce to the factory of Carlow, too far away to make it profitable for the smaller cultivators. For the sake of brevity, therefore, and due to its minor significance, we will skip the reference to the culture of beet and we will move now straight to the meadows, the last sojourn in our trip around the Irish landscape.

Irish farmers obtain the bulk of their fodder from the meadows, and this confers upon the work at the meadows an absolutely pivotal role in the local economic system. Although there is some contradictory historical evidence, it seems that hay making became popular in Ireland around the eighteenth century, when the demise of the preexisting seminomadic system of animal husbandry obliged Irish pastoralists to produce artificial fodder on a systematic basis (Evans 1957: 151–52). Similarly to what we have seen in the previous accounts, the process of hay making has also gone through radical technological changes. The grass is no longer cut by scythes but by rotary mowers, it is no longer turned by fork but by a hay-turner or haybob, and it is no longer saved in cocks but in bales made by the specialist machine. Still, once again mechanisation has not entirely eradicated the necessity of manual work. As

4. See Williams for rural England (1956: 149–50), and especially the more recent and fairly detailed analysis carried out by B.J. O'Neill in a Portuguese hamlet (1987: 147–59).

Evans reminds us: 'Today the baling machine is speeding up the process, but the bales, whether from the need of seasoning or from force of habit, are left piled in angular cocks scattered over the hayfield' (1957: 155). And here is where the labour demands of the hay harvest become critical.

To pile the bales of hay, at least two people are needed, a man to carry the bales – since they are quite heavy – and a woman or a child to hold them standing up while the 'cock' is being built. Although three people arc the ideal team for collecting the bales, theoretically a single man could do the whole job by himself, but it would take him much longer. We should not forget that even though the hay is already baled, a heavy shower could still inflict considerable damage, so it is better to do it as quickly as possible. Therefore, the more people that can be recruited for help the better. Furthermore, the hay harvest presents an interesting predicament as far as its social implications are concerned. Particularly when the weather has not been too good, the majority of the farmers will find themselves doing the same thing at exactly the same time, so that the possibility of getting a hand from other farmers is more restricted than ever, and therefore the necessity of maximising one's social contacts to provide for help in the hay harvest is stronger than ever.

We see from this that the hay harvest must have important implications as a catalyst for social engagements, all the more so if we consider how widespread hay making is among the farmers of the Three Districts: only 9 out of my sample of 65 do not cut any hay. Nowadays, however, a more modern alternative is beginning to compete with that old system of fodder production; this is the cutting of silage. The great inconvenience of hay was its critical dependence on the weather whims for drying the grass after cutting it. To make silage, grass does not have to get dry. There is no more need for sunny days (a terribly scarce good in the west of Ireland), since immediately after being cut the grass is stored in the silage pit and left there sealed with plastic for a couple of months or so to ferment, after which it can be used as fodder for the winter.

But silage cutting involves several problems as well. First of all, a silage harvester and a loading shovel are needed, both very expensive machines the purchase of which would only be profitable either for professional contractors or for big farmers with a reasonable number of acres to be cut every year. Secondly, a silage pit has to be built out of concrete, another big expenditure, even though farmers might get a grant from the government to cover a third of the expenses. Thirdly, a good number of people have to participate in the silage cutting, two of them, at least, skilled workers (one to drive the silage harvester and another for the loading shovel). As a result of all this, silage cutting is usually left almost entirely to professional contractors, who charge on average forty pounds per acre, far more expensive than the services of a hay mower, a haybob and a baler together. Furthermore, silage is good fodder for big cattle, but sheep and calves prefer hay.

The work at the silage cutting is a good example of a complex pattern of cooperation involving the use of heavy items of machinery. The contractor usually comes with the silage harvester, the loading shovel, the rotary mower and a few trailers, depending on how far the pit is from the field and also on how many trailers the farmer himself might bring, plus one driver per each one of those machines. The synchronisation and coordination between all the delicate operations involved in silage cutting is something delightful to watch. All the workers are usually fed at the farmer's expense, or maybe I should say at the farmer's wife's, who has to cook one big meal a day for all the men and take them sandwiches and tea up to the field twice a day. The close interconnection between household duties and farm jobs appears in silage cutting more visible than ever.

Even though it is almost twenty years since silage started to be cut, many farmers are still reluctant to take on silage production: 29 out of my sample of 65 never bother with silage, 27 combine both hay and silage, and only 9 rely exclusively on silage, which amounts to a total of 36 people engaged in silage cutting. The strong dependence on contractual work is what differentiates silage not only from hay but also from all the rest of the farm labour processes (see Leeuwis 1989: 63–64). Thirty out of the 36 silage cutters of my sample need a silage contractor, but this figure, though it is in itself high enough, has to be further qualified taking into account the huge cash expenditure involved in silage cutting, much higher than for the rest of the labour processes for which contractual services are needed. Neither hay nor silage is produced as commodities, at least on a regular basis.

With the cutting of silage our second ethnographic approach to rural Ireland comes to an end. This is what any farmer would tell if asked about the work on his farm. We have seen that the production of fodder in all its different components – grain, hay, silage – constitutes the basic aim of their work practices, together with a few items for human use or consumption such as turf and potatoes. It could be argued that to understand the real significance of fodder production we have to get out of this economy 'from the native's point of view'. The farmers of the west of Ireland cannot be reduced to their work practices. Let us see now what other insights can be gathered from a different standpoint.

3. AN ENQUIRY INTO THE ECONOMY

*T*he farming communities of the west of Ireland are in a process of rapid social change. In fact, they have been going through this process for quite a long time; but according to the people's historical memory, it looks like a relatively recent phenomenon. Everybody agrees that rural society is no longer what it used to be and, furthermore, that it will be no longer what it still is now. The past seems to be definitely lost in a cloud of confusing and contradictory accounts, idealised and abhorred at the same time. The future is imagined by means of current ideologies of modernisation that foresee urbanisation and industrialisation mercilessly devouring the traditional rural economy. And in between there is the ambiguous present situation, in which a persistently dwindling community of family farms strives to make a living amidst the esoteric dictates of the Common Agricultural Policy and the world economy.

It might be because of this uncertain panorama that the farmers of the west of Ireland do not seem to fit well into ordinary sociological and anthropological categories. To consider them equivalent to the fully fledged capitalist farmers from England, and maybe the eastern regions, would definitely be inaccurate; to see them on an equal footing with Third World peasant societies does not seem entirely appropriate either. It is true, on the other hand, that anthropologists working in Europe do not hesitate when it comes to defining their subjects as 'peasants'. But I have my doubts about the suitability of such a category with respect to western Irish farmers, even if it is just because they themselves use it only in a pejorative sense, both in English and in Irish. In any case, setting nominalist controversies apart, it is precisely this notion of liminality between capitalists and peasants or simply noncapitalists that will somehow constitute one of the basic points of my argument.

Our first concern is the economy as an intuitive notion. From this perspective, it appears as a specific domain of human activity deprived, apparently, of any social or cultural interference. The economy has to do with the hard facts of day-to-day subsistence and its inescapable rationality. If in the second chapter we saw the world of western Irish farmers 'from the native's point of view', that is to say, from the point of view of their work practices, now we are going to consider it through the looking glass of our own economic ideology.

I began by referring to animal husbandry as their most prominent work practice. Even though from a strictly empirical point of view it is land husbandry rather than animal husbandry that seems to absorb most of farmers' efforts and time, the work of the land is clearly subordinated to the requirements of the livestock, since land husbandry practices are essentially directed toward the production of fodder, be this corn, hay or silage.

To understand this unfolding of the work culture from animal to land husbandry, we have to go back to the sedentarisation of Irish pastoral economies, from the seventeenth century onward, since it is precisely the impossibility of moving the herds to new pastures that gives rise to the necessity of producing winter fodder through the working of the land. Thus, what for nomadic pastoralists turns out to be a *pattern of settlement* – nomadism as the main strategy to provide livestock foodstuff – for sedentary pastoralists appears as a *process of production* – the process of fodder production. It becomes clear therefore how critical the securing of food for their animals is for pastoral societies, be these nomadic or sedentary. I will return to this issue.

On the other hand, the dominant position of animal husbandry and its related agricultural practices in the work culture of western Irish farmers can be explained in terms of the demise of the old self-sufficient peasant economy, which brought about the specialisation in animal production and the parallel contraction of those work practices not related to animal husbandry but to the old self-sufficient sphere. However, as with the cutting of turf, the cultivation of potatoes, etc., that self-sufficient sphere cannot be said to have disappeared altogether.

The dominant position of commodity production in the farming communities of the west of Ireland is unquestionable; however, it is debatable when the process of commoditisation that led to the present state started to develop. The Irish sociologist Damian Hannan defines the agrarian economy of the west of Ireland before the Second World War as a natural economy, wherein 'little, if any, capital accumulation or substitution occurred [and] only part of the total exchange system was a monetised one' (1979: 33); Cuddy and Curtin maintain that, far from that, by the end of the nineteenth century the process of destruction of the 'natural economy' was well under way, so that 'the reproduction of farm households in the 1890s greatly depended on relations of commodity production and exchange' (1983: 181). Nevertheless, these two authors admit that 'except for the larger farms, the majority of households continued to produce "use values", agricultural and non-agricultural products for immediate consumption alongside their production of commodities' (ibid.).

It seems reasonable to assume that whether we define the agricultural economy of the west of Ireland before the Second World War as 'natural' or 'commoditised', both commodity production and the production of use values have been co-existing for a long time, probably since the British plantations (otherwise the English protectionist legislation of the seventeenth century against Irish exports would have been senseless).[1] What certainly must have changed ever since is the specific weight of each one of those spheres in the reproduction of the small farmers' economy as a whole. Nowadays, the sphere of self-sufficient production among western Irish farmers is much less significant than it was just twenty or thirty years ago. Turf cutting, a few potatoes, a vegetable garden, some hens and the odd cow to provide milk for the house are all that remain of the old peasant economy.

'People were so poor that they had to eat what they produced,' my friend Declan told me, 'they did not have the money to buy it, and if you don't have the money you have to do without it, as simple as that.' There

---

1. By the same time, however, Sir William Petty observed: 'Men live in such cottages as themselves can make in 3 or 4 days; Eat such Food (Tobacco excepted) as they buy not from others; wear such Cloaths as the Wool of their own Sheep, spun into Yarn by themselves, doth make their Shoes, called Brogues ... I may say, That the Trade of Ireland, among 19/22 parts of the whole people, is little or nothing, excepting for the Tobacco abovementioned, estimated worth about 50,000 l. for as much as they do not need any Forreign Commodities, nor scarce any thing made out of their own Village. Nor is above 1/5 part of their Expence other than what their own Family produceth, which Condition and state of living cannot beget Trade' ([1691] 1979: 76 and 82).

does not seem to be much regret for the loss of the time-honoured peasant self-sufficiency, which is associated with the poverty of olden times.[2] Some, like Noel, think that people got out of self-sufficiency when they started to get the dole, and they became spoiled then because they were receiving money for nothing, so they did not see the point in messing about with hens, pigs, vegetables and all when they could get food at the shop without effort.

But this 'self-sufficiency' has to be understood in relative terms. When people talk about self-sufficiency they refer in fact to the sphere of domestic economy run by women, which, to some extent, was no more than a residue of a wider market-oriented economic domain. Women would keep hens, ducks and geese, for instance, and people would certainly eat their own eggs, but much of the egg production was either sold or bartered for groceries. On the other hand, when after the Second World War the price of corn was kept artificially high, it gradually became more profitable to sell the corn than to give it to the hens and to sell their eggs. In other words, there is no point in being self-sufficient if you can get more food buying it with the money obtained through the sale of your produce.[3]

But there is something of a paradox in the demise of the old peasant economy. The concept of self-sufficiency can be used to refer to two slightly different things. I have just been talking about self-sufficiency as it relates to the early peasant society, that is to say, as it relates to the production of goods for human consumption without being previously commoditised. But the other meaning of self-sufficiency I would like to put forward refers to the production of goods that will not be commoditised either but that are for animal consumption rather than human consumption. And this definition of self-sufficiency is what in a way appears quite paradoxical, because the critical importance of fodder production as a self-sufficient sphere has come to the fore with the specialisation of western Irish farming in commoditised animal production; in other words, the self-sufficient sphere related to the production of goods for human consumption has gone to a secondary stage because of the increasing prominence of the self-sufficient sphere related to the production of goods for animal consumption.

2. 'Laments for old times are left to outsiders who need the strength and imagination of country people to save them from the decadence of their own society' (Glassie 1982: 493).

3. As a farmer put it to me very explicitly, 'now it would be too expensive to be self-sufficient.'

This type of production is a very important characteristic of Irish pastoral farming, in sharp contrast with other types of pastoral farming. Let me bring in now the example of Catalan stockbreeders and we might better understand why I put so much stress on the persistence of self-sufficient fodder production. The ecological conditions of the inland plains of Catalonia are not suitable for pasture. We will set aside now the reasons as to why in those conditions a stockbreeding economy has flourished in the last fifteen or twenty years; the significant fact to note here is that fodder production for Catalan stockbreeders takes place basically on an industrial basis.[4] Let us not forget now how important the provision of livestock foodstuff is for a pastoralist economy. The commoditisation-industrialisation of fodder production has reached such an extreme in Catalonia, together with a parallel process of supply monopolisation, that stockbreeders find themselves at the complete mercy of the fodder factories. The reason is an accelerating process of vertical integration, 'progressive' vertical integration as economists would call it.[5] This process has been triggered off by the gradual indebtedness of farmers to their fodder suppliers, who eventually appropriate the herds and from then on supply not only fodder but the young livestock too, in order to buy them back after a few months as fully grown animals. They are creating in this way a renewed version of the so-called 'putting-out system', well analysed by historians of proto-industrial economies. Therefore in a pastoral or stockbreeding economy the one who has the control of the livestock food supply, be this either pastures or artificial fodder, has in fact the whole society under his control.

The Catalan example demonstrates why it is so important that Irish farmers are still able to produce their own fodder. Now, as to the reasons that might account for this particular type of self-sufficiency, we might think that, in light of the counter-example I have taken from Catalan stockbreeders, they seem to be basically ecological reasons: Irish wet weather gives rise to rich pastures and to a lavish fodder yield. In fact, what we have seen for the west of Ireland applies similarly to the majority of mountain pastoral farming areas in western Europe, where we can find analogous climatic conditions. However, socioeconomic factors

---

4. Rees observed in 1939 (!) that large quantities of feeding stuffs were bought to supplement fodder crops by Welsh pastoral farmers, 'costing in some cases as much as twice the rent' (1950: 24).

5. See Davies 1980: 142 for different aspects of vertical integration in farming economies.

should not be neglected altogether,[6] such as the existence of a powerful domestic demand for agricultural products. This demand might stimulate a high degree of intensification of agricultural economies and, consequently, their deeper commoditisation and 'factorialisation', brought about by the necessity of using all sorts of industrial inputs (artificial fodder, etc.) so as to increase their output per labour unit.

This is a particular instance of what Van Der Ploeg has defined as 'externalisation', the process whereby an increasing number of tasks are separated from the farm labour process and reallocated to external agencies (1986: 34).[7] The extent to which fodder production has been externalised from the farm labour process among Catalan stockbreeders, and the disruptive effects that this has brought about, suggests the strategical importance of that type of production. It has strategical importance as a means of subsuming sedentary pastoralists to the rule of industrial capitalism through its full commoditisation and, vice versa, as a means of preventing that subsumption by keeping it away from commoditisation. If it is true, as Gudeman and Rivera have argued, that 'one of the puzzling features of the countryside is precisely that the house economy exists within a market context yet survives by avoiding purchases' (1990: 140), one could say as regards the west of Ireland that it has been by avoiding the purchase of fodder that the farming community has managed to survive.

The history of capitalism can be thought of as a gradual and expanding commoditisation of the economic system (cf. Hart 1982). If we imagine then a scale with industrial capitalism at one end as an instance of a fully commoditised economy, wherein even labour itself has become a commodity, and all precapitalists or simply noncapitalist systems of production at the other end, we could place the putting-out system of

6. According to Mann and Dickinson (1978), capitalism will not develop in agriculture because of the necessary tie of agricultural production to the seasons; production time (the time in which capital is tied up in commodity production) will be greatly in excess of labour time (the portion of the production period in which labour is allocated to creating value). This gap is seen to reduce the potential for profitable levels of capital accumulation in agriculture, thereby discouraging capital from investing in agricultural production (Buttel and Newby 1980: 19).

7. 'In contrast to industry, where a considerable part of the growing specialisation and division of labour takes place within the factory itself (and therefore does not imply a major increase in commodity exchange), agricultural development usually implies a process of externalisation which generates a multiplication of commodity relations' (Van Der Ploeg 1986: 35; see also Leeuwis 1989: 11 and 14–15 for the development of the derived concept of 'incorporation').

Catalan stockbreeders at one stage immediately before industrial capitalism, since in this case all the inputs of the productive process have been
fully commoditised except human labour, and somewhere before Catalan stockbreeders we would find pastoral farming in the west of Ireland.

The existence of such a sphere of noncommodity production triggers
a question that we will try to answer in the following chapters: under
what sort of social relations are its corresponding productive processes
carried out. These are not totally individualised, asocial, productive
processes but rather they take place in a particular social universe. It is
this social universe that will constitute the object of analysis of much of
the present research.

Let us first have a look at the following table, in which I have presented a schematic summary of the social bonds activated for the implementation of the labour processes we saw in the second chapter, on the
basis of the information I obtained in my sample of 65 farm families.

Table 3.1

The Labour Process in Its Social Context

	total	cont.	no cont.	nuclear	extend.	neigh.	no help
a.h.	65	53	58	34	24	21	7
turf	56	55	53	36	19	8	3
pot.	30	5	27	15	9	12	3
corn	37	34	19	6	7	9	18
hay	56	42	47	12	19	16	9
sil.	36	30	16	0	6	10	20

(cont.: contractual labour; nuclear: nuclear family; extend.: extended family; neigh.:
neighbours; a.h.: animal husbandry; pot.: potatoes; sil.: silage)

In the rows we have the different work practices under study: animal
husbandry, turf, potatoes, corn, hay and silage. In the columns we can
see the different types of labour used for each one of those. The first column shows the total number of family farms engaged in each task, in the
second we have the number of those who claim to use some form of contractual labour and, in the third, those who claim to use some form of
noncontractual labour. The fourth, the fifth and the sixth columns show
the different origins of those forms of noncontractual labour: nuclear
family, extended family and neighbours with no kinship relation. By
nuclear family I intend only wife and children of the farm manager, by
extended family I intend all those individuals related by kinship or affinity with the farm manager and who do not belong to the nuclear family.

Finally, in the seventh column I have recorded the number of family farms who claim not to use any type of noncontractual labour, so that the sum of the third and the seventh columns is equal to the first one.

For a correct interpretation of this table, it is necessary to point out that the information has been obtained not through direct observation of each one of those labour processes in each family farm (impossible for a single observer), but simply by asking each farm manager what sort of help he needs for each particular task. In other words, what the table shows is not so much how the labour processes are actually carried out, but rather how they are perceived by the respondent in terms of their realisation. I stress this point because it explains blatant cases of understatement or even misrecognition, such as that of the use of nuclear family labour for the silage cutting. We have seen how particularly important the help of wives was in preparing the meals on that occasion; many women told me that they abhorred silage cutting just for the extra work they had to do; and yet, none of the farmers interviewed recognised this as help for their labour process.

Although this is an extreme case, after carefully cross-checking this information with the data obtained through direct participant observation, I have noticed a certain tendency toward understating or misrecognising noncontractual forms of labour in general terms (cf. Hannan and Katsiaouni 1977: 84). This tendency clearly suggests the taken-for-granted character of that type of labour source – a key element to be taken into account in further analysis.

Let me underline the following point: the existence of this important sector of noncommoditised economic activities means that we are facing an 'economy' that includes its own negation – a nonmarket rationality. It is an 'embedded' economy, to use a familiar anthropological concept. But in this case, no matter how contradictory they might appear at the theoretical level, both market and nonmarket relationships seem to combine well with each other. We will see this next.

4. Tamed Commodities

*O*ur enquiry into the economy of western Irish farms has already disclosed the dichotomy between contractual and noncontractual forms of exchange. Let us concentrate our attention now on the first pole of this dichotomy. The following chapters deal with different aspects of what might be called the commoditisation phenomenon, as it relates to the productive processes of the farming community of the Three Districts. We will begin by looking at the world of commodities from its most apparent domain: the sale of farm produce to the rest of the economy. We will begin therefore not with the process of production as such but with the process of distribution.

If we were to write, following Kopytoff (1986), the social biography of a lamb, our account would result in something like this. It would start in the early months of the year, the lambing season, it would follow with the ensuing selection of those female lambs to be kept for replacement of ewes, and after four or five months it would end up at the sheep mart, the threshold of the conversion of our lamb into meat either for home consumption or for export. In the case of a calf, the process would be a little more complex. Probably the main character of our story would have been born among the dairy specialists of Co. Cork or Co. Kerry. Having not been picked up for replacement of cows, it would be immediately sold to a jobber who in turn would sell his stock to the small cattle breeders of the western region. There the calf would be fed and looked after for about two years when, grown into a bullock, it would see its first trip to the mart. A big eastern grazier might fancy the beast and buy it to fatten it up on his farm, or so might a cattle dealer, who again would resell it to the eastern farmer. The bullock might spend another two or three years in the rich pastures of the midlands before its second and last trip to the mart, and from there it would finally find its way to the factory. The resulting meat would have an 80 percent chance of being exported, the meat of a lamb slightly less (Sheehy and O'Connor 1985: 59). If it did not end up in an Irish supermarket, it would have a 55 percent chance of going to Britain, 30 percent to other EC countries and 15 percent of finishing its social biography outside the EC (McAleese 1982: 277).

This pattern of livestock circulation has been going on, with some modifications, practically since the specialisation of Irish agriculture in pastoral farming, from the second half of the nineteenth century onward (Gibbon 1973: 494). At the beginning, the dependence on British markets was virtually absolute (see Arensberg and Kimball [1940] 1968: 25ff). In fact, it was only with the entrance of Ireland into the EC (1973) that non-British markets started to become relevant for Irish agricultural exports. Nowadays, however, the whole system of exchanges built up around livestock and livestock products has been decisively altered by the so-called intervention policy of the EC. This policy was an attempt to prevent the dangers of over-supply by buying up the surplus of certain agricultural products such as beef, milk and others with EC funds allocated to each of its national governments for such a purpose. Those surpluses had to be frozen and eventually dumped into Third World markets as soon as the prices became conveniently high. But this system did not go all that well. Corruption came to the fore when it was discovered that EC funds had been diverted to favour certain meat factories at the expense of others according to the political criteria of the government. Furthermore, the fact that surpluses grew much faster than the money available to buy them, together with the collapse of the Middle East markets due to the Persian Gulf crisis of 1991, has discouraged EC policy makers from pursuing their policy of intervention much further. As a result, local markets were flooded, giving rise to much of the present crisis in western Irish agriculture.

These matters are constantly mentioned in the conversations of the farmers of the Three Districts, because the majority of them are perfectly aware of their position in the general system of the world economy. They also claim that their function as store cattle producers has made them suffer the worst consequences of the crisis. When cattle are too plentiful and the prices are so low, it works out cheaper for the eastern graziers to buy older beasts. So the small breeders of the western region have to keep their cattle for two or three years now, when before they could sell them after only one and a half years. They, therefore, have to run with the expenses of keeping their cattle longer without getting any profit for it. Furthermore, as Declan Kennedy pointed out to me, 'the calves are very delicate after being born, they can die from the most little thing, and if your calf dies you will not get your money back. But once they are big enough they become as hard as a rock; they won't die then unless they are neglected. So all the risks are for the small farmers of the west and all the money for the big lads of the east.' (cf. Curtin 1986: 73).

We can see therefore that the farming communities of the west of Ireland are no more than a little ring in a long chain of commodity exchanges that interconnects all the spheres of the capitalist world economy. Let me repeat, if from a strictly ecological point of view, sedentarism is what defines pastoral farming in the west of Ireland as opposed to other forms of pastoralism, from a socioeconomic perspective, commoditisation is what differentiates Irish farmers from any type of self-sufficient system of production, whatever kind this might be. What I will try to do in the rest of this chapter is to present the sociocultural scene of commodity transactions in their mediatory role between the farming community and the wider social system, that is to say, commodity transactions that involve the sale of the final farm produce. This description is meant to emphasise the characteristics of the social relationships that operate on the liminal space between the two different social universes encapsulated in the farm world and the capitalist system.

Until approximately twenty years ago livestock were sold and purchased mainly at the fairs, held regularly in all the main towns of rural Ireland. When the farmer decided to take his cattle to the fair, he had to set out the night before since it was very important to arrive there as early as possible. A lot was at stake in that dangerous night trip: any accident could make the farmer lose the work of years. All the animals had to be blessed before being taken to the fair, and the driving of cattle to the fair was surrounded by all sort of 'strange' beliefs. One of them, for instance, refers the first person encountered during the trip. It was thought to bring very bad luck to meet a woman first of all. To prevent that, a farmer whom I know used to send one of his sons ahead so that the latter would be the first person he met (cf. Evans 1957: 260–61). Once in the town where the fair was going to take place, the cattle invaded all the streets and the negotiations with the dealers started.

Although fairs represented not only an occasion for economic transactions but also for general social intercourse,[1] farmers do not seem to
have very good memories of them, at least as far as their economic side
is concerned. They felt that they were always in the hands of the dealers,
who could pay whatever they wished, whereas the farmer never knew the
real value of his stock. That is why the Irish Farmers' Association has
championed marts against fairs since its inception in 1955 (Curtin and
Varley 1982: 349). Nowadays marts have entirely replaced fairs as the
primary mechanism for the commercialisation of livestock.

The mart is now the basic institutional framework of commodity
transactions in the farming community. Not all transactions take place
at the mart, but certainly the most important of them do: those associated with the sale and purchase of livestock. At the mart the process of
exchange has been radically altered. The mart is a cooperative owned by
the creamery and with a parallel system of capital holding (see Chapter
8), the aim of which is to organise the sale and purchase of cattle and
sheep. Now the stock is not spread all over the streets of the town but
enclosed in pens at the mart premises and sold by auction. All animals
are weighed before being sold, indicating to the auctioneer what price
has to be taken as a base to start off the bidding. The buyer does not pay
the farmer directly but the mart; he is not allowed to take the cattle until
he pays the whole price, and then the mart pays the farmer. The difference between the price the farmer gets and the price paid by the buyer
makes up the profits of the mart, which are used to pay the employees
and to cover general expenses. As in the case of the creamery cooperative,
no dividends are ever distributed.

Modern means of transport have made redundant a great deal of the
lore associated with the final trip of the livestock. To take the animals to
the mart, some hire a truck from a contractor; others do it themselves if
they have a big trailer or they do not have too much stock; others get the
loan of a neighbour's trailer; and still others just throw their beasts into
someone else's vehicle. Whichever way the farmer brings his stock to the
mart, he likes to be there early in the morning. Even though the pen that
will be auctioned first is decided by lot, farmers do not waste their time
when it comes to getting their animals, especially cattle, in the pens.
Sometimes they even go the night before and leave the animals there
with a bit of hay, thus they do not have to rush the following day.

1. 'The fairs were formerly organised in a recognised sequence of goods and livestock, terminating in sports and horse-racing – and not infrequently in bloodshed'
(Evans 1957: 255).

Similar to the fairs, the mart still constitutes a stage both for social interaction and economic exchanges. When the sales have finished, the pubs of the town become packed with farmers talking over their pints about how bad the price of the stock is, making arrangements for the sale of a few bales of straw or a few bags of corn and so on. The mart as a social occasion provides a platform for the activation of the internal networks of the farming community. But apart from this, the mart itself, in its more strictly economic function, enforces upon its visitors a whole set of social and cultural practices somehow evocative, in a sort of condensed fashion, of the external relations of the farming community, the relations of farmers with the rest of the society.

I once saw a sheep dealer inspecting lambs in a pen, a particularly dirty place, with his tie hanging over and 'cleaning' the back of the beasts as he stooped now and again to touch them. It is a hilarious image that may suggest the dichotomies of the two cultural systems that intersect at the mart: the farm world on the one hand, and the capitalist economy on the other, of which the cattle and sheep dealers can be said to represent a noticeable committee. It is not difficult to spot them among the crowd, usually dressed in suits, hats and long coats, in sharp contrast with the peak caps and casual clothes of the farmers. When the auction starts, in the case of cattle, all the dealers get together at a particular corner of the ring where the animals on sale are exposed; opposite them sits the auctioneer; and on his left-hand side there is a little cabin, a sort of telephone box with a tiny window on top of it, from which the farmer who is selling his stock can look at the scene without being seen. For the sheep auction it is a little different: the auctioneer goes from pen to pen followed by the crowd, in which buyers mix indiscriminately with farmers. But in both cases the functioning of the auction is much the same, and the cryptic language used on the occasion is also the same. Only after a good few days of observing attentively the group of buyers during the auction did I start to take notice of the tiny little movements of their heads or their fingers to communicate their intentions to the auctioneer. It was one of the most compressed communicative codes I have ever seen.

And yet, this is a relatively 'explicit' sphere of communication. Much more secretive is the language used in the surreptitious world of collusion practices. 'Once I brought twenty-five lambs to the mart,' a sheep farmer told me, 'and I put them in pens of fives and sevens, to make them look nicer, you see, but a fellow came along and got the whole lot for a miserable price, there was plenty of people around but nobody bid against him. It wasn't fair!' Collusion takes place first and foremost among livestock dealers; it is commonly known by the expression 'making rings', and it simply means that in certain circumstances buyers do not bid against each other but have previously distributed the livestock lots among themselves so that they can pay whatever they wish with no competition. It seems that these practices are particularly widespread in the case of sheep: if you see a man sitting for a long time in a pen reading the paper, you can be sure that he is 'hatching' the pen. Nobody will bid against him when the auction starts.

Joe Moran, the cattle auctioneer, who happens to be a part-time farmer as well, told me that only professional dealers make rings, those who get their profits just from buying and selling and are thus interested in buying cheap rather than good cattle. But the farmer who buys store cattle to fatten them up wants good stock and will pay any reasonable price for it, taking no notice of rings. A different philosophy of commodity exchanges seems to inform the attitudes of professional dealers. 'Dealers look at buying and selling collusion,' Curtin and Varley argue, 'as a means of introducing order into something otherwise inherently disorderly. By accepting collusion as intrinsic to their ability to buy cheaper and sell dearer, dealers stand out therefore relative to mart authorities and farmers for the deviant conception of legitimate means they hold and practice' (1982: 355). In any case, what seems clear is that collusion practices have to some extent subverted the initial aims of the livestock marts, which was to preserve the ideal of free competition between buyers and sellers against the notorious inequalities developed at fairs.

But are farmers totally defenceless in the face of the buyers' rings? There is also collusion among sellers. The most common method is to have a friend bidding for your stock just to put up the price; maybe you can give a few pounds to a buyer you know to bid for your stock even if he is not interested in buying it. This is absolutely illegal and anyone who is caught doing it is severely sanctioned by the mart authorities. But sometimes, when the prices are bad, the auctioneer might turn a blind eye (remember that he is a farmer) and, furthermore, he might even put up the price himself, pretending that someone is bidding. Nevertheless, there are some problems as regards the feasibility of those practices.

First of all, to bid for your own stock you have to be an expert, farmers say; you have to know how the prices are going, for example. And the majority of farmers who go to the mart maybe only twice a year are not up to date with the state of the market prices. Secondly, as Curtin and Varley have argued, even though the mart is a cooperative owned by the farmers and run by their representatives, they will also turn a blind eye and a deaf ear to evidence of collusion among dealers because marts to survive have to compete among themselves to attract dealers (1982: 356). 'The buyer is the boss,' a farmer commented to me. 'If they are not happy they will not come, and then there is no mart and everybody would lose.'

On the other hand, if the farmer suspects that there is a buyers' ring going on, or he is simply not happy with the price he is getting, he can always turn down the sale of his animals. When the bidding has started, the farmer has to indicate to the auctioneer whether he agrees with the last offer. If he does not, the animals are not sold and the farmer can take them back; if he is happy, then the auctioneer shouts 'on the market!' and from then on the highest bidder is the one who gets the stock. But again, this is no more than a formal prerogative that overlooks the actual circumstances of the seller, that is to say, how badly he might need the money.

And what about skipping the mart? Is it possible for farmers to sell their stock somewhere else? When I first went to the Three Districts, in the spring of 1990, a group of sheep farmers was trying to organise a cooperative for the transportation of lambs directly to the meat factory of Kilkenny. 'In this way you can cut out the middle men,' they were saying. But not everybody was fully convinced; others argued that the meat factory will never pay you the whole price because they also want to protect the interests of their own middle men, the representatives they send to the livestock marts to buy animals for them. For the cattle, on the other hand, the meat factory is practically out of the question for the majority of small breeders. You need big cattle for the factory, four years old at least, whereas the small men can keep their animals only for one to two years.

A different matter altogether would be the purchase of calves. Unlike what happens with the sheep and lambs, all dry cattle farmers have to buy their calves, even those who keep suckler cows, since the milk yield of a good cow can feed on average up to three calves. They can go to the square of Athenry or Mount Bellew, where jobbers display the calves they got from the dairy farmers of the south. Sometimes those same jobbers come along with their trucks up to the farm itself, which is what Declan Kennedy preferred; he said that when they come to sell you are at an advantage, 'it's them who want to sell, you didn't call them at all,' but if you go to the square then it is the other way round, 'very cute people, very cute.' But Tony Dolan, another small stock breeder, said that when the jobbers come over with their trucks they put the animals in such a way that they all look very nice, but you don't know what you are buying really, you don't know the weight, you know nothing, so it is much better in the square, he concluded.

And would it not be possible to buy calves directly from dairy farmers? Certainly it would, but we are entering into a different sphere of commodity exchanges, those that take place within the boundaries of the farming community. We will talk about this aspect in Chapter 7.

We see therefore that there are different ways of commercialising one's livestock, although the mart is without doubt the most important of them all. From the point of view of the general economy, it could be said that the sale of livestock, in whatever circumstances it might take place, turns into a social category what thus far has only been the object of individual work practices. But this is not the case from an anthropological perspective. Unlike what political economists would argue, from the anthropological point of view this transition into the social does not stem from an abstract category of naked individual production, which acquires its social uniform only by the very fact of being sold and bought in the capitalist market. Far from this, that 'individual' process of production appears as socially clothed, maybe not in the elegant smoking jackets of the free-market economy, but in the more informal track suits of interhousehold cooperation.

The mart is the point of intersection between two cultural spheres and, for the same reason, it is at the mart where the dual character of livestock, as far as its social nature is concerned, becomes most apparent (cf. Gray 1984). If we look at livestock as the result of a productive process, we can see that it constitutes the definitive object, from an economic point of view, not of a set of individual practices, but of the social processes *internal* to the farming community; but if we look at livestock as a commodity, as the starting point in a series of commodity exchanges, we will realise that it embodies by the very essence of its commodity form the vital link of the farming community with the outside world, that is to say, it constitutes the definitive object of the social processes *external* to the farming community.

In this chapter we have seen the way in which we can say that a farming community is no more than an appendix of a wider socioeconomic system. The important point to stress here is that the connection of the farming community with the external world takes place almost exclusively through a particular type of social relation: commodity exchanges.[2] It could not be otherwise if we think that the external world is dominated by a capitalist economy whose main attribute is precisely the

2. Almost exclusively through commodity exchanges perhaps with the exception of public taxes and, in years gone by, the landlords' rents.

commoditisation of its productive processes. The essential characteristic of this type of exchanges is that they take place between anonymous subjects on the one hand, while on the other they involve immediate and pre-determined counter-services. That is what I call the contractual principle of social transactions. That the relations of the farming community with the rest of the social system have to be regulated by such a principle can be justified thus not only because it is the dominant principle of the capitalist economy, but also because its defining characteristics, anonymity of the parties and immediacy of returns, fit in particularly well with the notion of social distance that separates the farm world from the capitalist economy; in other words, with the fact that farmers and stock dealers can be seen, to some extent, as 'moral aliens'.

This separation is precisely one of the things I would like the reader to keep in mind after having gone through this chapter. The cultural framework of the type of exchanges that take place at the mart clearly insinuates this idea of alienation. Farmers and stock dealers hold contradictory interests; they are at the opposite ends of a moral continuum. Collusion practices in particular and the whole notion of opposition between two antagonistic worlds, which so clearly define the socio-cultural atmosphere at the mart, indicate the same direction: a contract, an exchange of commodities, takes place 'where communities have their boundaries, at their points of contact with other communities, or with members of the latter' (Marx [1867] 1976: 182).[3] In what follows we will see the ways in which the principle of contractualism articulates itself with different degrees of 'otherness' and how this affects the essential characteristics by which I have defined that principle.

---

3. Cf. what Evers and Schrader (1994) have defined as 'the traders' dilemma' to refer to the contradictions between the market ethos and community values.

5. THE MORAL BOUNDARIES OF FARM WORK

*I*t could be said in one sense that the farmers of the west of Ireland constitute a moral community. By this I do not mean that they are all in the same moral community; probably there are as many moral communities as neighbourhoods and as many as individual farmers, endlessly overlapping one with the other. Moreover, each individual farmer might define himself the centre of different types of moral communities. Still, no matter how diffuse the boundaries of such moral aggregates are, or how obscure and ambiguous its constitutive principles, there is a sense in which some of the social relations that farmers entertain are pervaded by a certain feeling of social distance, of 'otherness'. It is of different intensity according to the type of social encounter in which it crops up; sometimes it seems to melt away with other principles with a stronger constitutive capacity, but sometimes it stands out with particular clarity, providing the social relation wherein it appears with a specific character.

My aim now is to deal with the representations of two marginal identities among the western Irish farmers I met. This discussion can be seen as an attempt to come to terms with the slippery question of different cultural identities from what could be called a situational point of view, that is to say, from the point of view of their implications in the constitution of the specific type of social relations in which they become relevant.

Unlike the British and many other Europeans, the Irish have had very little contact with non-Western people. Maybe that was the reason why the day that two black Africans came around the Three Districts selling some clothes, panic was general among the women of the parish.

'Those blackies are mad for white girls,' I heard them saying, 'for them it is a way of going up, you know, they are very bad.' That was certainly an extreme case of racial shock, and very unusual in a country like Ireland which, with the possible exception of the north, is relatively homogeneous from the ethnic point of view, taking into account that there is practically no immigration. But the feeling of otherness in its most radical expression, 'racial otherness', is by no means absent.

When I joined in the potato harvest of Tomás Reegan, I soon realised that the majority of the potato pickers were looking at me suspiciously; I could not extract many words from them. 'Do you like this type of work?'; 'I do not'. 'What do you do while you are not picking potatoes?'; 'Nothing'. At the end I became so desperate that I decided to give up any attempt at communication. 'Your workers did not seem to be very chatty,' I said to Tomás a few days after the harvest. 'Oh, well, they are travellers, you see, one of them was dead afraid when he saw you with the camera, he thought you were going to show his picture in the dole office!' 'We tried to persuade him', Tomás went on, 'that you were just a student doing research and that you had nothing to do with the dole crowd.' No good, he did not turn up any more.

That was my first meeting with the elusive Irish tinkers, the nomadic people of rural Ireland. The tinkers are hired for the picking of potatoes every year on a more or less regular basis. The deals are made with the eldest one of them; they include the days of work and the pay per acre. He will then have to recruit as many helpers as he thinks convenient to work under his orders. Sometimes, the pay is not per acre but per amount of potatoes picked. In this case, empty bags are usually left alongside the drills at a distance of so many yards from each other so that the pickers can throw in the potatoes as they pass. Each picker then gets his pay according to the number of bags filled. Although this system of hiring workers has the advantage of encouraging competition among the pickers, it also presents the disadvantage of encouraging fights among them about who has been filling this or that bag. Whatever the deal might be, there is always bargaining in the price. One time Tomás told the head of the group that the price should be reduced since he had been picking potatoes as well, but the tinker replied that one of his lads was moving the tractor when this was supposed to be Tomás's job, so one thing made up for the other. 'Tinkers are very smart, you can't fool them.'

If there is any clear instance in which the feeling of otherness among western Irish farmers acquires a notorious prominence, it is in the dealings with the tinkers. Sometimes they are improperly called gipsies, for the similarity of their ways of life. But the ethnic origins of the tinkers are unclear; they probably come from old peasant families evicted from their lands. Traditionally, the tinkers have been coexisting with Irish farmers in a more or less parasite/symbiotic relation. They used to get from them all sorts of trash, straw, horse hair and car batteries, and they would offer in exchange metal works such as buckets and gates (hence their name). The hardest and dirtiest of the unskilled farm and house jobs, such as picking potatoes, pulling beets or cleaning chimneys, were usually reserved for them as well (see Gmelch 1977: ch. 2). Nowadays they live mainly on unemployment benefits.

My second encounter with the tinkers was shortly after the potato harvest. A middle-aged man, with a young boy of about ten, driving a red van full of gates, called on the farm of my friend Noel while we were dosing the cattle. Noel was polite to him, but he did not buy anything. 'Better not to have any dealings with these people', he told me afterward. 'They come to your farm and start to look whether they can take something, and then they might rob you and beat you up. They are very crafty; they live on their brains while other people live on books. This is their strategy for survival, it is very hard to catch them. But perhaps those who came today were very respectable people, I don't know', Noel admitted.

'Oh, sure they can be respectable,' a farm worker points out to me, 'but I don't like them; and, I tell you, they are happier than you and me. They can draw the dole from different counties, you see, because they have no identification. At one time they were offered houses by the County Council in Tuam; some used them and some didn't, and after a while all the houses were in ruins.' 'But some of them might be very respectable families', he repeats now and again. 'They used to be a poor decent crowd,' says a farm woman, 'going back years they used to do bits and pieces for the farmers and they would live on what the farmers would give to them, a bag of potatoes and things like that; but since they got the dole, they became kind of vicious.' 'The dole is a very bad thing', an old bachelor comments to me. 'Look at those tinkers, they don't have to work because they draw the dole, that's why they are vandals; it's very bad to give money for nothing.'

Fear, suspicion, distrust, apprehension and a certain paranoia, define the attitudes of farmers and rural people in general toward the itinerants. My hostess, an in-marrying woman from another parish, used to let in a tinker girl now and again for a cup of tea. When her husband came to know what was going on, he immediately forbade her to do it again. Next time a group of tinkers called round selling gates, she had already learnt her lesson: 'When I saw them with their red hair I got a fright, I didn't even open the door; they are dangerous, you know.' Any misdeed done in the parish will be almost automatically attributed to the tinkers. My next-door neighbour lost his two donkeys; they were found some weeks later a few miles down the road, but in the meantime a group of tinkers who were camped in the surroundings got the blame. When the rectory was robbed after the weekly collection, nobody had any doubt that the tinkers had something to do with it; much the same when an old solitary bachelor was assaulted and his dog killed after having sold a few cattle at the mart.

They say that tinkers are predominantly red-haired, even though it seemed to me that there was no golden rule to identify them. Maybe a biological anthropologist could detect some physical peculiarities resulting after so many generations of in-marrying. But the people of the Three Districts have not the slightest knowledge of biological anthropology and yet they can recognise a tinker on the spot.

'Look at those, they are tinkers,' a friend of mine warned me while a group of girls was approaching us. 'How do you know they are tinkers?' I asked. 'Listen to their words, rough way of speaking, look at their faces, the way they are dressed, don't you see something different from the rest of the crowd? Don't say anything when they come near to us! They have eyes in the back of their heads.' There is something that singles them out, but my friend could not tell me exactly what. He insisted on their peculiar speech, always using short sentences, and referring to you as 'boss'; he also mentioned some of their characteristic surnames: Ward, Sweeny, Moriarty. 'The dog, you see, the dog we had years ago, he could identify them straight away, he knew when the tinkers were coming and he would never let them in.' Interestingly, he also admitted that there is a woman representative of the itinerant people in the County Council of Galway, 'but she is very educated, you would never say that she is a tinker.'

The point I am trying to make here is that no matter how strong this feeling of otherness is in the contacts of the tinkers with the settled community, it has never pulled them apart entirely. On the contrary, as I said earlier, the tinkers have traditionally provided farmers with different goods and services. And still now they constitute a significant supplement to the farm labour for certain tasks, the dirtiest and most unskilled of them all. This work is not very important at the present moment, since the mechanisation of the process of production and the decline of tillage farming has done away to a great extent with the necessity of hiring unskilled workers. Historically, however, the use of unskilled farm labour was an indispensable condition for the reproduction of the farming communities of the west of Ireland, especially seasonal farm labour (see Breen 1983).

This brief acquaintance with the Irish tinkers has served me to suggest the association of the concept of otherness with the implementation of the lowest tasks in a farm. The fact that these are often allocated to individuals from other ethnic groups is by no means peculiar to Irish farmers. In my fieldwork among the Catalan stockbreeders of the plains, I came to know that for the last decades they have been employing Spanish-speaking workers quite regularly, although lately these have started to be replaced by North Africans. Among the fruit cultivators of the coast the use of black Africans as labour power for their farms has become very widespread in the last few years, especially before the press reported on the over-exploitative conditions to which they were subjected.[1] All this could be seen as a particular instance of the more general trend, common both to industrial and to agrarian economies, that points to a degree of ethnic mobility among the lower classes higher than among the better off. But I am also tempted to wonder to what extent such ethnic division of labour stems from the fact that a farming community, as long as it sees itself made up of equal individuals, needs to allocate a culturally different person to those tasks the performance of which by a member of the community would clearly undermine that image of equality.

In what follows I will concentrate my attention on the representations of another 'ethnic minority', the one that in years gone by had been supplying the farmers of the Three Districts with the bulk of their unskilled labour power. These were the Irish speakers of the Gaeltacht communities of Co. Galway popularly, and quite pejoratively, known as 'culchies'.

An old bachelor said to me once that there is something wrong with Irish: 'There are things you cannot put an Irish name to, you cannot say New York in Irish!' What is the use of having a language with such awkward shortcomings? 'What good was Irish to me,' a young Irish-speaking woman told me. 'I know a lot of people back in my place with no Irish and they got good jobs, and they didn't have a word of Irish. What was the Irish good for? We all had Irish [she refers to her family] and it got us nowhere. In the factory I was working the manager had no Irish.

1. Similarly, in his analysis of labour relations among American farmers, Kimball referred to Mexican labour employed on a seasonal basis (Arensberg and Kimball 1965: 124).

Why did he get there? Because he had a pull! When people said to me why is it that I did not teach Irish to Fergus [her son], I say that Irish is no good to him. I would be happy if he could pass an exam, that's all you need; he is going to pick it up anyway, the same as we picked up the English. When I went to Galway to work in a hotel for the first time, I and a friend of mine, we had very little English because our school was all through Irish. We did not let on that we had no English and we managed well. But I know that my parents feel a bit ashamed of not having English'. (Incidentally, while she was talking to me she was wearing a T-shirt with the following inscription: *'Leabhair Béarla liom … agus brisfidh me do phus'* [speak English to me and I will break your face].)[2]

There is an interesting homology in Co. Galway, and I think this could be extended to many other regions of western Ireland, between the quality of the land and the language spoken by its dwellers. The better the land is the earlier the Irish language was forgotten, and vice versa. A homology that, on the other hand, also has strong reverberations in Irish political history, since the present ruinous state of the Irish language bears a clear testimony to four hundred years of colonial oppression (see Ó Fiaich 1969).

The decline of literary Irish goes as far back as the British plantations of the seventeenth century, when the native Gaelic gentry and their ancient bardic schools were wiped out by the conquerors. English then became the language of political power and the upper classes. In fact, the Irish word for English, *Béarla*, originally meant something like 'technical' or 'official' jargon (Foster 1988: 122). But for the illiterate poor, the majority of the population, the Irish language was still the only means of communication until well into the nineteenth century. By then two important circumstances had contributed to the spread of English among the lower classes. One was the establishment of the National schools after 1831; the other was the Famine (1845–9), which struck disproportionately the Irish-speaking population, both by its immediate lethal consequences and by its long-term effects, pushing thousands of families toward America and England (Wall 1969: 86–87). 'To have good English,' a farmer commented to me, 'has always been our passport to emigration.' From then on, the number of Irish speakers has been

---

2. At the beginning of this century, the playwright J.M. Synge wrote about the Aran islanders: 'In the older generation that did not come under the influence of the recent language movement, I do not see any particular affection of Gaelic. Whenever they are able, they speak English to their children, to render them more capable of making their way in life' ([1907] 1979: 85).

halved practically at every generational replacement. At present, no more than one percent of the population of the Irish Republic live in the Gaeltacht, the districts officially recognised as Irish speaking, but it is reckoned that there are only 8,751 people with sufficient attachment to the Irish language to be able to transmit it to their children (*Irish Independent*, 24 April 1990).

If we were to draw a comparison with the history of the Gaelic cultures in the other 'internal colonies' of England, Wales and the Scottish highlands, we would realise that the reason for the demise of the native languages cannot be pinned down exclusively to political domination. 'On a popular level,' Foster observes, 'spoken Irish faded far more quickly than the native languages of Scotland, Wales or Brittany. This was an indication of disruption, penetration, settlement and commercialisation, rather than a result of government policy' (1988: 122). Even so, I do not see how disruption, penetration, settlement and commercialisation can be too neatly separated from the consequences of specific government policies. Be this as it may, what I would like to stress now is that the overall social context within which the deplorable history of the native Irish culture has developed is responsible to a great extent, in my view, for the gradual stigmatisation of the Irish-speaking population among the farmers of the Three Districts.

It is understandable from the history of the Irish language why it has become a low prestige speech among the rural population. All the more so the closer that population is, in time and space, to Irish-speaking communities – since the knowledge of Irish among the educated urban middle classes might acquire a different meaning altogether: a token of cultural distinction and 'ethnic' consciousness. No matter how hard the successive Irish governments, since the proclamation of the Irish state, have tried to turn back the history of the Irish language, no matter how hard they have worked at trying to impose its use on the whole population, there does not seem to be any way of getting rid of that enduring legacy of their colonial past: the English language. Even their latest efforts simply to preserve the tiny Irish-speaking communities from utter extinction have done very little to alter the crude socio-economic reality of the Gaeltacht districts, hardened after so many years of political grievance. And therefore, they have done very little to rectify the contempt that so many Irish people feel for their native speech. 'The only good thing we got from the English,' a farm woman said to me once, 'is the language.'

The people of the Three Districts started to forget their Irish about three generations ago, although some scattered Gaeltacht pockets still remained for another few decades. When I arrived, only the old folks could remember a few words they had been able to pick up from their Irish-speaking parents, despite the stern determination of the latter not to pass any Irish on to their children.[3] But the core of the Irish-speaking population in Co. Galway has been, probably since the early years of independence, around the far western shores, in the region of Connemara, surely one of the poorest farming areas of western Europe.

That the Irish language has been better preserved in the worst lands is nowhere more apparent than in Connemara. Tiny little fields broken down by their characteristic stone walls, packed with bulky rocks and surrounded by huge extensions of bog land. Green, grey, brown and the profound blue of the sea combine to give rise to an absolutely fascinating scenery for anyone but its inhabitants, who for so many centuries have been eking out a living from a landscape suitable only for contemplation. 'The more distant background of the communities which remain today in this conspicuously unfavourable environment lies in centuries of invasion, destruction and recovery' (Brody 1973: 46). Invasions and destructions that endlessly pushed the native population toward the west, their last refuge against their greedy eastern neighbours.

Under those conditions, it is not surprising that agriculture can be only one of a number of income and product sources that integrate to form the household economy (Kane 1979: 142). Nowadays, after the tourist boom of the sixties, together with the government-sponsored industrialisation of the western regions and different types of subsidies for Irish-speaking communities, the people from Connemara have been able to keep up with the living standards of the rest of Irish rural society. But until recently, there was still a remarkable gap between the two, which could be precariously filled, as the *Gaeltacht Report* of 1925 already pointed out, only through different secondary sources of income. Seasonal migration was prominent among them (Brody 1973: 69).

The seasonal workers from Connemara used to sell their services at the fairs that were celebrated in the main rural towns of the County. The nearest to the Three Districts took place in Athenry, approximately six miles to the east of Galway city. Not long ago, every year after the winter months, the central square of the town used to get particularly busy on Sundays. It was not a fair day for cattle or sheep but for another type of commodity: the labour power of the Connemara seasonal workers.

---

3. Wall refers to the traditional 'barbarous cooperation' between parents and teachers to prevent children from learning any Irish (1969: 86).

48

Any farmer who needed a couple of strong arms to give him a hand in cutting turf, sowing or digging potatoes, making cocks of hay, reaping corn, pulling beets, or any other exhausting task, would go down to town at that time, where those poor men were hanging around with their bags of clothes and maybe with their spades too, waiting to be hired. The farmer would inspect them 'as if they were cattle,' farmers themselves admit, and having gone through the customary bargain he might reach an agreement with one of them to work at his farm for a couple of weeks. A pint in the pub would seal the deal, 'and sometimes you would not see the likes of them after that.' But usually the two men would then go back to the farm, either in the farmer's sidecar or walking. Once there, the farmer had to feed and shelter his labourer as long as required, and pay him the agreed salary afterward.

Not for too long would the seasonal worker stay with the same man; although they were good strong workers, it was not always easy to manage them. They might have a row with the farmer and then they would go with someone else, but the next season all was forgotten and the farmer was very likely to take the same man back again. In fact, what they normally did was to spend all the summer going from farm to farm doing bits and pieces here and there, until they might meet a solitary bachelor with whom perhaps they would stay for the rest of the year.

Why a bachelor? Farmers say that those fellows from Connemara were really rough, and they used to get drunk every week-end; whereas a man would take no notice of that, women did not fancy having such a crowd hanging around for too long. 'Oh, they were very strong, very strong men, but they were treated like blacks. That was slave work, I tell you, some of them couldn't even see the village until the week-end, working all day long and sleeping at night in the hay shed or wherever.' And the majority had no English at all, maybe just a few words; an old man tells me that he used to call his Irish-speaking mother when he wanted to talk to his worker, so that she could translate for him what he was saying.

Unlike the tinkers, the culchies had the reputation of being very hard workers; their status was certainly not as low as that of the itinerant people, but they were nonetheless considered to be quite dirty, vicious, and sometimes a bit stupid, 'although no way you could mislead them' despite their poor English. There is a mixture of contempt, fear and a certain pity in the feelings farmers express when they talk about their seasonal workers from Connemara. As a matter of fact, they recognise that their violent and intimidatory behaviour was the only way those poor men could defend themselves against the inhuman conditions under which they had to work. With the Connemara crowd kicking around, very few locals would venture into the village on weekends. They used to get drunk and were very fond of drawing their knives, especially against those who laughed at their broken language.

All that was twenty or twenty-five years ago; now the demand for seasonal work has practically disappeared thanks to the process of mechanisation, apart from the odd job for the tinkers. On the other hand, many of those Irish-speaking workers came over only to get 'a bit of education', that is to say, to learn English, so that they would end up in the building sites of London, Manchester or Birmingham, where they could certainly get better wages. And furthermore, there is plenty of money in the Gaeltacht now, farmers of the Three Districts assert with some resentment; they have subsidies, tourism, and the dole, so there is no need for them to come over for work any more.

We have seen thus how these two marginal groups, culchies and tinkers, are represented by the farmers of the Three Districts, and from this we cannot fail to notice that major differences between those two representations crystallise in diverse forms of social categorisation, which in turn refer to diverse strata of the emic social scale. Still, I believe that from the previous account we can also recognise important analogies between the two. Both social groups participate in a certain degree of 'otherness', very clear in the case of the tinkers, less so with the Irish speakers. There is one way in which none of them can claim to belong to the community of farmers, not so much, certainly, as an occupational category, but rather as a moral aggregate[4] within which there is a specific code, a system of rights and obligations, that does not apply to strangers. As Long has observed among central Peruvian farmers, occasional wage labourers always come from outside the community precisely because 'the entrepreneur, it seems, attempts to segregate his dealings with them from sentiments of kinship or community which might create additional obligations on his part' (1986: 92).

Here we have a very important clue to the understanding the type of social relation that links those outsiders with the farming community: the contractual relation. It is the same relation that we saw linking the farming community with the outside world at the mart. It is a relation by

4. In a Castilian hamlet, S.T. Freeman observed that: 'Next to Gypsies, the most despised groups are migrant herders and itinerant tradesmen or farm hands, for they are assumed to live outside the context of sedentary – and thus "civilised" – society' (Freeman 1970: 179–80).

definition impersonal and universalistic, a relation that turns out to be particularly appropriate in dealing with those individuals who fall outside the system of rights and obligations that exists only within the boundaries of the farming community, once again, as a moral community.

And in this way we have taken another step in our attempt to unravel the social framework within which the farm labour processes are carried out. From what we have seen here and from what we saw at the mart, we know by now a particular social context in which the use of a contractual relation appears as a perfectly rational option and, conversely, the use of noncontractual relations would seem definitely out of the question. It is a social context defined, to a great extent, by the feeling of otherness among its participants. This means that in the interaction between the social categories of individuals we have been observing, otherness plays a major role in justifying the appropriateness of a contractual relation. But it does not mean that contractual relations take place only between total moral aliens.

Nothing could be more flexible, ambiguous and indefinite than the notion of social or moral distance. In the following chapter we are going to look at two further examples of economic relations organised on a contractual regime. The element of otherness is not completely absent but it appears in combination with other circumstances that explain the persistence of a contractual link. At the same time, the decreasing social distance between the contracting parties deeply affects the nature of their transaction.

6. WORKERS AND MACHINES

*M*y friend Pat told me once that not too long ago, there were three classes of people in Ireland: the upper classes, the farmers and the workers. The upper classes would not mix with the farmers nor would these mix with the workers, who were considered second-rate citizens. It would have been very unlikely for an upper-class boy to put an eye on a farm girl, never mind a working-class girl, although it would not have been seen as bad as the other way round (an upper-class girl going out with a farmer's son or a worker). And the same applies to the relations of farmers with workers; farmers would not mix with working-class girls, nor would it have been socially acceptable for a farm girl to marry a working-class boy. Nowadays things are not so strict, Pat explained; workers can be as well off as farmers, and the majority of farmers are getting off-farm jobs anyway. It is all mixed up now. But he still thinks that farmers are quite endogamic, and this is a matter of education, he says; only a farm girl could put up with a farmer's way of life. 'Say a man coming from the fields into the house with his boots full of muck, and leaving his wet stockings to dry at the fire … Ah! a towny could not stick to that, she would not survive a single day on a farm.'

Shortly after Pat told me that, we were shearing the sheep with his part-time worker Joe Murphy. Our bodies were dripping with sweat when we went into the house in the afternoon to have our dinner. As usual, we took off our boots before going into the kitchen, where Kate, Pat's wife, was laying the table. 'Oh!, the smell of your feet is awful!' she said to Joe, 'I can't stick to it, it has ruined my dinner!' 'That's good for you,' Joe replied, jokingly but a little embarrassed; meanwhile, Pat was devouring his meal without paying too much attention to what was going on. After Joe went, she made me open the window and the door of the kitchen, 'the smell of his feet, didn't you smell it?, it was awful.' Kate had been living in a farm since she was born, and she was of course well used to the farmers' way of life, but maybe not so well to that of farm workers.

Pat has full confidence in his worker and friend Joe, despite his wife's anxieties. Joe Murphy is the son of a retired postman who also farms twenty acres of land. He used to live with his parents and two other brothers until he got married, when he moved to a caravan. With such a small farm, none of the brothers has much interest in knowing who might eventually inherit the land, as all of them have had to look for off-farm jobs. Now Joe works on a part-time basis for Pat. There is nothing Joe could not do at the farm, Pat told me. In fact, I have not seen any fixed pattern of division of labour between the two of them, except perhaps just a slight tendency for Pat to take on the jobs of more responsibility. Obviously it is always Pat who decides what job is to be done next and by whom, but the two men openly discuss the best way of doing it. I have never seen Pat protesting against Joe's work, or shouting at him (something that, incidentally, happens very often when Pat is working with his son). Every Saturday evening Joe receives his pay and disappears until the next Monday morning.

According to the last population census for the Three Districts (1986), only 8 people out of an agricultural working population of 207, which includes both self-employed and assisting relatives, define themselves as 'agricultural employees'. There is no doubt that farm workers as a class, in the ordinary sociological sense of the word, no longer constitute a significant element in the social structure of western Irish rural communities. This does not mean, however, that nobody works on a farm for a salary any more. But the situation of the present farm workers in the overall social structure is a little more complex than what may be suggested by a simple dichotomy farmers/labourers, a complexity that escapes the shallow insights of any statistical method.[1]

1. As a matter of fact, the class of landless farm workers was never very prominent in the Irish rural social structure. Only after the Famine, once the former cottiers had been practically exterminated, did a class of landless labourers start to take shape, always a minority, however, in comparison with the much bigger and politically active tenant class (Clark 1979: 121–22 and 211ff). After the Second World War, not even that minority could survive the process of mechanisation (McNabb 1964: 209; cf. Breen 1983), with the exception perhaps of those working for the big eastern farmers.

The impression one gets when studying the life histories of farm workers is that they constitute a kind of 'residue' of the social structure: those who come from unproductive farms seem to be more likely to end up selling their labour power either to agricultural contractors or directly to their bigger neighbours, normally until they manage to obtain a better job in town or they simply emigrate. Farm wage-work never signified a real alternative to industrial wage-work elsewhere; instead, it should be taken rather as sort of putative training school for one's future social settlement.

Even though farm work is for most people just a temporary experience, there is a certain possibility that farm workers might to some extent reproduce themselves *as a class* for more than one generation, especially in those cases in which they happen to inherit the tiny family farm – and, therefore, they are not very likely to emigrate. But according to my data, usually a man who inherits a very small farm either remains a bachelor all his life, so that he does not reproduce himself socially because he fails to reproduce himself biologically, or, especially nowadays, he gets an off-farm job, so that he might reproduce himself biologically precisely because he fails to reproduce himself socially.

Whatever the chance they have to reproduce themselves, it is important to point out that not all farm workers come from tiny farms. There is another element that, together with the already mentioned lack of economic viability of the smallest farms, accounts for the existence of farm workers in terms of 'social residue'. In an impartible system of inheritance, such as that prevailing in rural Ireland, at every generational replacement there is a breed of men with no access to the means of production, and therefore, a breed of potential sellers of labour power, wherever it might be that they manage to realise the value of their vital commodity. The fact that they have been disinherited from the family land makes them represent their social condition of labour-power sellers as a direct result of their landlessness, that is to say, as a direct result of the prevailing system of inheritance; and this is *irrespective of how big or small the farm of origin happens to be.*

The world of farm workers comprises another social universe in which the use of some form of contractual relations for the organisation of farm labour makes sense. There is an important difference here from what we saw in the previous chapter. Now the element of otherness has faded away until it has practically disappeared altogether. I began by quoting my friend Pat's reflections on the old endogamic practices of the farm class as regards the workers. I documented immediately afterwards an episode in which a certain feeling of class prejudice might not have been completely absent, and I have ended up by referring to farm workers as a simple stage in the life cycle of the majority of farm men. It could be argued that the immediacy of returns that characterises all contractual dealings fits in particularly well here, not so much because the parties involved belong to different moral communities, but rather because of the *shifting condition* of the majority of farm workers, which makes them unsuitable for any type of long-standing relations with undefined counter-services.

The universalistic and anonymous character of contractual relations appears much less definitive in so far as the element of otherness has been practically abrogated in this new context. An all-pervasive personalism seems to lubricate now the junctures of an otherwise cold and distant monetary exchange. In what way, we could wonder, does this new element of personalism agree with the requirements of the farmer/worker relation? From what we saw in Chapter 5, one would have thought that it was precisely distance rather than closeness that farmers were looking for in their interaction with their employees. Students of rural societies, however, have profusely indicated the specific advantages of particularistic relations in the organisation of agricultural work (e.g. Williams 1956: 39). As Newby has pointed out: 'The small scale solidarities of the farm-centred community help to ensure that the relationship [between farmer and worker] is rarely stripped down to the cash nexus and that any conflict which may arise is put down to a clash of personalities rather than a product of the system' (1977: 340).

That the blending of the cash nexus between farmer and worker with all sorts of extracontractual ingredients increases the possibilities of exploitation, or that it helps to water down the antagonism between employer and employee, may explain why it appears more advantageous for the farmer to get around the impersonal treatment that goes with all commodity exchanges. But the simple fact that it is handy for the farmer to interact with his worker on a personal basis does not account for the emergence of that particular type of interaction. Furthermore, have we not seen as well a context in which the same legal form was used precisely to magnify its universalistic and anonymous character?

It is to the nature of the labour process that we have to turn if we want to find a more satisfactory explanation. In talking about the tinkers and culchies, I underlined the fact that it was the most unskilled of the farm tasks that they came to perform. Conversely, in my account of Joe Murphy's work I remarked on his high degree of involvement in any type of farm job, sometimes practically on an equal footing with the farmer himself; there is nothing Joe could not do at the farm, Pat recognised. The mechanisation of the agricultural labour processes has very much increased the work autonomy and responsibility of the farm worker. In stark contrast with what has happened in industry, where new forms of machinery have dissolved the labour process conducted by the worker and reconstituted it in terms of technological discipline (Thompson 1983), in agriculture the same impulse toward technological development has given rise to the opposite result: control over the farm worker has become more and more problematic.[2]

We should not put too much emphasis on the social implications of this process of mechanisation, though. There is no evidence that before the technological revolution the interaction between farmer and worker was less personalised.[3] Still, it seems to me that the characteristics of the different labour processes that have to be implemented on a farm reverberate quite strongly in the constitution of their corresponding social form. And that is the reason why, in my view, the universalistic and anonymous character of all contractual relations has to be removed in the particular case of that which links farmer and worker, but without questioning, on the other hand, the very contractual nature of the relation, especially with respect to the immediacy and certitude of the counter-services exchanged, virtually inevitable given the ephemeral existence of the farm worker's status in the west of Ireland.

It is worth pointing out, however, that the identification of the worker with the farmer stems not so much from any psychological affinity between the two but from the very nature of the social relation that links both of them, formalised in the contractual form and substantiated by the different tasks the worker is supposed to perform. Even in those cases in which there is a particularly outstanding familiarity and intimacy between farmer and worker, interest and emotion seem to be well mixed but never confused. Let me bring in a very simple incident that took place between the farm worker Seán Fahey and his employer Noel Forde, two men who can be said to be on very good terms.

I was having tea in Noel's house when Seán called. He came to arrange the milking of the cows for the following day, since Noel had been invited to a wedding and he did not have anyone to do the job for him. The two men started to talk very freely about different topics,

---

2. 'Such is the work place autonomy of the modern agricultural worker that the maximum degree of identification with the employer beyond the size of the pay packet becomes a matter of real financial importance' (Newby 1977: 419).

3. I must thank Rosemary Harris for drawing my attention to this important point.

much in the line of the friendly mood that characterises their relationship. Seán was saying that he had recently visited a big dairy farm in the east with many full-time workers. 'They were very good, everyone knew well what he had to do, no one had to give any orders, and no complaints!' He compared that with his frustrating experience in the sugar factory, where he had been employed for thirteen years, and where there was always someone protesting about the smallest thing! When Seán went, Noel commented to me that Seán had never liked the factory: 'Seán is too good for the factory; he said that once the manager rebuked him for working too hard since he was making a fool of the rest, would you believe it?' Noel put the blame on the damn unions, which seemed to have the economy of the whole country under their control.

Only a few days later, I met Seán at his home. He did not seem to hesitate in the slightest when he was recalling his good memories from the factory, the best job he had ever had, he repeated now and again. It is not that he was openly contradicting what he had been saying in front of Noel a few days before, but I could not fail to notice a radical change of mood in the way he was talking about factory work, in his emphasis on how clean it was compared with the dirty and mucky farm, on the good money he had earned. He did not mention any conflict he had ever had with the manager or with his fellow workers. I do not take Seán for a hypocrite or for a crafty story-teller; I would simply say that he knows very well the difference between his subjective, personal, feelings and the objective personalism involved in his relation with his employer.

The point I would like to stress here is how this objective personalism disturbs, or even subverts, the contractual nature of the bond that links farmer and worker in many of its presumed essential characteristics. As has been suggested, it is the decreasing social distance between farmer and worker that accounts for this form of subversion of the spirit of contract. In what follows we are going to look at the same phenomenon but in a different type of social relationship. We will leave the world of farm workers and we will concentrate on the relationships between farmers and agricultural contractors.

In a context of small family farms, it is more common for farm workers to work for an agricultural contractor rather than for the farmers directly. Agricultural contractors are those who possess the heavy items of machinery that are needed nowadays to carry out most farm labour processes. An agricultural contractor hires his services to the farmers for cutting silage, baling hay, sowing corn, etc. and employs in turn two or three workers to drive his machines. From a formal point of view, both farm workers and agricultural contractors share the same legal form in their relationships with the farmer. But from a more substantive perspective, there is a sense of social hierarchy between farmer and worker, no matter how minimised the social distance between the two might happen to be, a sense of social hierarchy that is entirely absent in the relationship between farmers and contractors.

The complexity of the relations of a contractor with his clients stems from the different kinds of factors that bear upon them. We have the specifications of the farmer-contractor settlements. There is secret dealing, Noel told me, between a farmer and his contractor; if other people knew about that dealing it could damage the interests of the contractor and the farmer himself. Some farmers who have good machinery might agree with the contractor to help him out, lending him an extra tractor or a trailer, in exchange for a discount in his fees. And together with these more or less explicit and particularistic arrangements, there are all sorts of implicit provisions that are taken for granted in all relations of a farmer with his contractor. The feeding of the workers, much to the women's anger, figures prominently among them. 'This is only in the west of Ireland,' some farmers' wives complained to me. 'They say that in the east they bring their own food, but here we are more backward!' Another thing normally understood as well is that the contractor will never ask his fees straightaway, rather he will wait until the farmer has been able to realise the value of his stock. Since most of the sales do not take place until October and November, this means that a contractor can be kept waiting for between three and six months before he is paid for his services.

Apart from the specifications of the negotiations as such between farmer and contractor, other more 'external' circumstances also have to be taken into consideration, since they reverberate in turn into the nature of the social relationship formalised in those dealings. When the timing of the operation is of crucial importance due, for instance, to ecological factors, such as is the case with corn cutting, a further bond of trust is built up on the bare contractual agreement. A farmer who needs to hire somebody for the performance of a particular task will never just chance it. If he does not know anyone right from the beginning, he will ask a neighbour whether he knows somebody who can do that job well: it is always better to have some references first. But the dependence of the farmer on the contractor is also reversible, to the extent that a man who wants to do contract work but who cannot count on a network of potential clients, be this based on neighbourhood or any other circumstance,

does not have the slightest possibility of success. A very common strategy for newcomers into the business is to buy the machinery from a
retiring man and to 'inherit' from him his network of clients.

Highly valued is the man who sticks to the same contractor even if
somebody else is offering him a cheaper service, and even if he cannot
get the contractor at the time he wants him. It is not their fault, farmers
say, you can't help it because everybody wants them at the same time
and, furthermore, they can be delayed for the smallest thing, so you
shouldn't blame them. 'The word in the west of Ireland is very important,' Noel told me. 'A man has to stick to his word and has to be proud
of his word.' Once you have a good contractor you'd better not change
it, he explained, even if you meet a cheaper one, because next year things
might be different and then if you want to go back to your first man he
might not come. If you always stick to the same man, he will not let you
down. In other words, if you always stick to the same man, you have the
right not to be let down. Because it is parallel to the high regard given to
the faithful customer, an equivalent opinion is held about the contractor
who remains loyal to his clients, again especially in the face of apparent
economic disadvantages. However, this is not a simple case of opposition
between moral principles and economic interests.

Pat Sheridan used to always get the same man to spread the lime on
his beet field. But one year when Pat did not have much to spread there
was no way he could get him to do the service; he was making excuses
all the time. Eventually, he told Pat that he did not think it profitable to
come over for such a small amount of lime. Pat deeply resented the attitude of his contractor and he decided not to call him any more, no matter how much lime he had to spread. It is not that Pat does not consider
the importance of economic profits – quite the reverse, in fact. The same
day he was telling me that a man asked him at the mart whether he
could sow a few turnips for him. But Pat had his seeder ready for the
beets, it takes an awful lot of work to change it over again, and for the
amount of turnips that man wanted it would not have paid to do it. So
Pat told him straightaway that he would not do the job for him.

Pat explained all that to me to demonstrate that his resentment
against his lime contractor did not stem from the fact that he does not
understand or does not approve of the primacy of economic interests,
but that it was caused by the dishonest behaviour of the contractor,
making false excuses to delay a commitment he knew he would not fulfil. Interestingly enough, on the other hand, irrespective of the personal
grievance Pat could feel on that occasion, he also criticised the attitude

of the contractor in terms of his objective lack of economic rationality. 'I don't know if this is good business,' he said referring once again to his contractor's behaviour, 'but I don't think so. The next year I had plenty of lime to spread but I wouldn't call him at all.'

After that, Pat started to use the services of his second cousin (father's father's brother's son's son) for the spreading of the lime. No matter how many different ways I asked him whether the fact that the contractor was his kinsman provided him with any advantage, he did not seem to put any importance on it, 'he just happens to be a relation, that's all.' He even said that should a neighbour turn up with a better price, he might move on to him. But he immediately added that probably it would not be worth doing because he does not have too much to spread; moreover, now that he has been with his second cousin for years, he knows well how much he needs and when he needs it.

Do material advantages penetrate kinship or other type of social relationships so deeply that the language of economic rationality takes preference over moral justifications? Noel was telling me that once he used the services of John Costello's bull to inseminate his cows. When the job was finished, John said that his bull had inseminated eleven cows, whereas Noel was absolutely sure that there were only ten. Noel thinks that John was well aware of the number of cows; it is not that he was trying to get a few extra pounds adding a non-existent cow to the bill, he just wanted to create an argument that would spoil the cordiality of the dealing and so he would not have to pay the luck money, a token of friendliness and goodwill given by the seller to the buyer as a recognition of fair play (see Chapter 7). Again, Noel dismissed John's attitude in terms of its lack of economic rationality. He defined it as 'crafty', as opposed to what he thinks a 'good businessman' would have done. John knew that Noel was just starting his dairy business at that time; he should have realised that it was to his advantage to keep on good terms with Noel in view of possible future dealings instead of engaging himself in a silly discussion for the sake of a few pounds. 'But John does not look at it in this way,' Noel observed scornfully, 'he is just a peasant.'

We see from this example that the ethical wrapping of the farmer-contractor relationship is not just a moral tie to be respected even against the possibility of economic profits. On the contrary, both Pat and Noel argued explicitly that it was precisely the long-term material profitability that in fact justified the moral behaviour in the short term. As Bloch has pointed out in his excellent analysis of the economic significance of moral relations: 'Morality is adaptative where maximisation would not be' (1973: 85). We will see another instance of this dichotomy between the economic and the moral in a later chapter.

But there are other qualifications to the relation of a farmer with his contractor. Another circumstance that bears conspicuously upon such type of dealings is what we could call the professional status of the latter. Thus far I have been talking about contractors and farmers in general terms; it is important now to make a further distinction.

A contractor is more often than not a farmer himself who has decided to invest his money in buying machinery to make an extra profit going on hire for other farmers. But the extent to which that extra profit is merely a sideline to the farm or, conversely, has become the main source of income, draws an important distinction between two types of contractors. On the one hand, we have those who are in the business on a devoted professional basis, we might say. They possess the most sophisticated agricultural machinery and always have farm workers at their service. These men might have a small amount of land themselves but they are never, for obvious reasons, very big farmers, otherwise they would not be able to cope with their two jobs. The cutting of silage and corn are the farm tasks for which they are mostly required.

On the other hand we have those who might possess the odd machine and who might sometimes go on hire for their neighbours, but never on a regular basis. They do not necessarily have to be small farmers, since their contract work is subsidiary to the farm enterprise, and they never have employees working for them. The jobs for which they will be hired depend on what kind of machine or machines they have; it can be anything really: baling hay, digging potatoes, ploughing or harrowing a field, bringing stock to the mart. Unlike the first type of contractors, who might have a very large network of clients, these other people very rarely work other than for their immediate neighbours.

Still, these are just the two poles of the scale, two ideal types, we might say, since the majority of cases fall somewhere in between. The more confused the condition of these contractors is with that of the rest of the neighbouring farmers, i.e., the more their contract work is subsidiary to the work they do in their own farms, the less 'pure' the contractual agreements they make with their clients. Why is it then, we could wonder, that they still choose the impersonal contractual relations to deal with their very neighbours? Could they not rely instead on the more informal mutual aid system so characteristic of neighbourhood interaction?

I will devote the next chapters to the complexities of these types of relations among farm families. For the moment, the only thing I will say is that there does not seem to be any straightforward answer to this question. Some people maintain that a monetary payment is required when machinery is involved, while others argue in terms of the costs for the person giving the service – the higher those costs, the more likely a contractual agreement. On some occasions, farmers deliberately avoid calling on their neighbours for particular jobs they could very well do, either in terms of immediate or delayed returns, and they prefer instead to rely on a stranger. That is the case, for instance, of Declan Kennedy, who always uses the artificial inseminator for his suckler cow when he could get cheaper and more effective services from his neighbour's bull. 'There is a lot of hassle in bringing a bull,' he told me.[4] On some other occasions, by contrast, it is precisely the opposite: Brendan Moran had been dealing for several years with two different contractors for the cutting of his turf and corn, respectively, but when Eamonn Murphy started on the business, Brendan moved on to him straight away: 'he is a neighbour, you see.'

Furthermore, as has been suggested, for the same type of job different forms of payment may be acceptable. John Moyles engages two different neighbours for the cutting and baling of the hay. Sometimes he pays them in cash, but it is by no means uncommon to exchange work too, so he might well go with his trailer to draw a few bales of hay or sods of turf for them. But at this point it seems to me that we are already crossing the boundary between the contractual principle and that of an entirely different social universe.

As we saw with the case of farm workers, the minimisation of social distance between the contracting parties embroils the nature of the contractual relationship. It is as if the cold spirit of contract started to melt away when confronted by the warmth of face-to-face interaction. The overlapping of neighbourhood with the status of agricultural contractor blurs the distinction between balanced and generalised reciprocity, between immediate and delayed returns and, certainly, between neighbours and strangers. Even if some form of monetary exchange is involved at some stage, this can no longer be taken as the real payment for the

---

4. In a Catalan community of the Pyrenees, Codd has observed that peasants prefer to sell their milk to the cooperative rather than to other villagers: 'They prefer the impersonal transaction to the personal one with the claims and counter-claims it involves' (1971: 204).

counter-service provided. As a farmer put it to me: 'I always give a few pounds to those who come to help me out, but they don't do it for money, really; it is as a sign of appreciation more than anything else.' Money loses its material value as it is endowed with symbolic power, the power to stand for an absolutely different type of social relationship.[5]

5. 'Where it is not seen as a separate and amoral domain, where the economy is "embedded" in society and subject to its moral laws, monetary relations are rather unlikely to be represented as the antithesis of bonds of kinship and friendship, and there is consequently nothing inappropriate about making gifts of money to cement such bonds' (Bloch and Parry 1989: 9). A final qualification should be added. The fact that a man doing a job for a neighbour does not receive as much as he would if he was selling his service in the open market does not mean that what he gets has a purely 'symbolic' value. I would say that it has both values, material and symbolic, inversely correlated. The more money one gets when working for a neighbour, the less it can be taken as a representation of a parallel relation of good neighbourliness, which might level out in the long run an immediate asymmetry, since the very material value of money compensates the emergent imbalance. Conversely, the less money given to the neighbour, the more it has to be considered as a token of further transactions. As Bloch has argued: 'Immediate reciprocity is tantamount to the denial of any moral relationship between the parties while delay between gift and counter-gift is an indication of the moral character of the relationship … we can, however imprecisely, estimate the amount of morality in a relationship by observing the degree of tolerance of imbalance in the reciprocal aspects of the relationship' (Bloch 1973: 77).

7. The Community Through Monetary Exchanges

*I*n the previous chapters I have been dealing with the contractual principle as it applies to the buying and selling of farm produce outside the farming community, and to the hiring of farm workers and the services of agricultural contractors. In all those instances, the contractual principle could be said to go hand in hand with some form of 'otherness' or social distance between the parties. Neither livestock dealers, farm workers, nor agricultural contractors are 'farmers' *strictu sensu*. But, quite obviously, it would be mistaken to conclude from this that this form of social relationship applies only when farmers are dealing with people with a different occupation. The applicability of the contractual principle should not be related to the fact of not belonging to the farming community as an occupational category but rather as a *moral community*. In other words, the farming community as an occupational category is only partially coextensive with the farming community as a moral community. This means that there are people who belong to the farming community as a moral community but who are not farmers, and that there are people who are farmers but who do not belong to that moral community.

Yet as has been shown in the previous chapters, the correlation of contractualism with moral or social distance does not appear as a simple matter. Farmers who exchange commodities between themselves are not necessarily 'moral aliens', in the same way as not all farm workers or agricultural contractors fall outside the boundaries of the farmers' moral community. In this chapter I consider the principle of commodity exchanges not as the nexus between the farming community and the overall economic system, which was dealt with in Chapter 4, but in its internal constitutive capacity, and in its capacity to impinge on the social structure of the farming community itself. We will shift our attention once again to the process of distribution.

The production of commodities is deeply rooted in the history and traditions of Irish rural society. We only have to look, for example, at the set of beliefs associated with money and the rituals accompanying the sale of major goods to confirm the long-standing importance of monetary transactions in the reproduction of Irish farming communities. It is often the case that behind those rituals of exchange there is the belief in the magic power of money, the power to endow its carrier with 'good luck'. When after a long bargaining period there seems to be no way of reaching an agreement between buyer and seller, the difference, if it is small enough, might be turned into 'luck money'. Thus the buyer will pay according to the seller's offer but he will get back the difference as luck money, which is not supposed to be spent lest the good luck associated with it be lost.

In some other instances, it seems that it is not money as such that carries good luck but the condition it represents. If a farmer has to make an important purchase, he will try not to pay with his own money but to borrow from a close relative. The reason for this is that he would be afraid of losing his good luck if he paid out of his own resources. Now, since the debt has to be repaid, and the farmer will have to give away his own money, it could be argued that he will lose his good luck all the same when he returns the borrowing. But this is not the case; there is no danger of losing one's good luck in returning a borrowed sum since, by rights, it is not one's money that is being relinquished but the lender's. At the end of the negotiations, the situation will be the same as if the farmer had paid the purchase out of his own pocket, but it could never be said that he has given away 'his' money.

One would be tempted to interpret these old customs not only as proof of a deep-seated culture of monetary transactions but also of the danger that might surround such transactions. Certainly, the more commoditised a farm economy is the more it is at issue when its final product reaches the threshold of the market and, consequently, the more that final transaction is likely to be embedded in clusters of beliefs that otherwise would seem to hinder the normal course of commodity exchanges. All the more so, we could add, when the decisive sale takes place in a situation of face-to-face contact between seller and buyer and of relative defencelessness for the first, such as that, for instance, of the livestock fairs that we referred to in Chapter 4. But in fact those practices used to take place not only at the livestock fairs, that is to say, at the point of transition between the farm world and the wider social system, but also, and especially, among farmers themselves, in the monetary transactions internal to the farming community. In this sense, Hugh Brody maintains that they should be interpreted as symptomatic of the particular social context within which they take place: 'Behind them lies a concealed assumption that dealing is inimical to friendliness, and therefore to community. The more developed and widespread such practices are, the less ascendant the pure motive of profit; again they are clues to a traditional mentality' (Brody 1973: 197).

We will leave aside Brody's idea of the absence of profit-maximising attitudes in what he calls 'traditional mentality'. The point I wish to make here is simply that commodity exchanges not only materialise the connection of the farming community with the rest of the society, but they also represent a constitutive principle of the farming community itself, and the farming community understood not only as an occupational category. We know that the production of a farm can be either commercialised or devoted to self-sufficient purposes. But within the category of commodity production a further distinction should be made between what goes outside the farming community itself, the final produce, and what remains within the boundaries of that community. In both cases we see the operation of the contractual principle; in both we are dealing with commodity exchanges, but they take place in absolutely different social universes.

Let us have a look now at the production of hay. We have seen that most farmers produce hay for their own use. It is by no means uncommon, however, that at the end of the year many farmers might find themselves either with a surplus of bales or with a deficit and, as a result of it, a circuit of exchanges will be activated to even out those final imbalances. This is apart from the fact that those who do not bother cutting any hay always receive a few bales from their neighbours. These exchanges can either be monetary transactions or they might involve different types of counter-services. A man who does not have much help for drawing the bales gets in touch with one or two neighbours he knows are interested in buying hay; they reach the following agreement: the neighbours will give him a hand with the bales and in exchange he will sell them a few slightly cheaper.

Another example of internal commodity transactions can be taken from the selling of calves by dairy farmers directly to dry-stock breeders. I have already stated that there are very few dairy specialists, so that the majority of them keep their calves to rear as dry stock. But it is amazing how reluctant farmers are to engage in this sort of dealing with their neighbours. They say that there was more of this buying and selling of stock among farmers years ago, but now with the tuberculosis controls nobody wants to take the risk. But even the dairy farmers themselves who might have some calves on offer do not seem to trust their neighbours as possible buyers. Noel Forde, who is a big dairy specialist, sells most of his calves to a jobber. However, he might sell the odd one to a neighbour. Once he did it while I was around, and he was not paid straightaway. 'There is no problem with this man', he told me, 'because he is an honest man. But it is dangerous not to get paid on the spot because them calves are very delicate animals, they can very easily die and then it would be difficult to get your money.' Once he sold a calf to another man for a hundred pounds and the man told him that he would pay him the following Saturday at the local pub. When Noel got there, the other one put the money into the pocket of Noel's jacket. Noel did not check the money at that time, and when he went home he realised that he had only eighty pounds. He was so angry and so ashamed of himself that he did not even dare to tell his wife about it.

But perhaps the clearest occasion on which commodity exchanges appear in their constitutive capacity can be seen at the corn harvest of the bigger growers, those who produce a marketable surplus. Corn for foddering and straw for bedding, thatching or foddering as well are used by the majority of farmers, but let us not forget that out of my sample of 65 farm families, 28 do not grow any corn and, on the other hand, there are 13 who claim to sell surplus. Furthermore, similarly to what I have said for the hay, deficits and surpluses might crop up among different self-sufficient growers at the end of the season. To compensate for the deficits of the community in general terms, both structural and conjunctural, a stream of commodity exchanges flows every year from its corn fields. Dealings are made in pubs, at the mart, by phone, or simply through advertisements in the local press. Unlike what we saw with the contractor's services, here there is no necessity of a trust relation between buyer and seller; anyone who happens to have a few tons of corn or bales of straw for sale will do. And yet, it cannot be said that such transactions take place in the social vacuum of a pure contractual agreement.

Séamus Murphy's corn harvest can be taken as a good example. Even though he is not a big farmer, he happens to sell most of his corn harvest. I met Séamus on a sunny Sunday afternoon in late August, when he was trying to sell a combine harvester to my friend Pat Sheridan. Séamus is Pat's mother's brother's wife's brother's son, although the two men call themselves 'first cousins'. Séamus has sixty acres of land, but he spends most of his time working in a pub in Dublin -whose owner, incidentally, is Pat's sister's husband. Thus far, Séamus had been able to keep the farm thanks to the neighbours' help, looking after the land and the stock while Séamus was away, but in the end he thought it better to get rid of it together with the farm machinery he still had, including the old combine harvester Pat was interested in.

The combine was at the time reaping one of Séamus's barley fields – there are no holy days when it comes to doing such urgent jobs as the corn harvest. Since he cannot mind much livestock, most of his corn production is for sale, both to a merchant and to several neighbours who come along as soon as they hear the noisy mechanisms of the combine at work. The buyers arrive with their trailers full of empty bags and wait for their turn near a sort of big hopper into which the combine keeps throwing loads of grain. From there the grain is released into the bags the buyers have brought in. The bags full of corn become awfully heavy and it is practically impossible for a single man to carry them up to the trailer, but anyone who happens to be around will give a hand.

First, there are the different buyers themselves waiting for their turn to get their load, like Tommy Duggan, one of Pat's neighbours who got the loan of his trailer for the occasion. Together with them we have people who came to have a word with Séamus to see when he would go to cut their corn, such as Pádraig Joyce, a dairy farmer who also happens to be Séamus Murphy's father's sister's son and Pat's mother's brother's son. Others, on the other hand, might be some simple passers-by with not much to do on a Sunday afternoon, like a flock of children who were unpacking empty bags and tying them up once filled. And there were still others, like Pat, interested only in having a look at the combine, and myself, interested only in nosing about as much as possible. Even someone's relatives from England, on holidays for a few days, had also been persuaded to help out.

'Here we all help each other, the same as with the threshing,' one of the corn buyers pointed out to me while I was ingenuously enquiring about the rationale of those work exchanges. A rich mixture of contractual relations, kinship ties, good neighbourhood relations and an all-pervasive generalised reciprocity seemed to model the social landscape in Séamus Murphy's field that Sunday afternoon.

But the social interaction brought about by the commoditisation of corn does not finish with the grain harvest. A few days after the cutting of the corn, the straw is ready for baling, and a new crowd of customers will congregate shortly afterward at the corn fields again. Let us see what goes on in Pat's farm on this occasion. For the baling, first of all, Pat gets the loan of a baler from his first cousin and neighbour John Collins. This year he is selling straw to ten different people. Some of them are old customers, like two brothers from Mayo whom Pat met a few years ago at the sheep mart. The two of them come every year and take two full lorries of bales. Another old customer is Willy Walsh, Pat's mother's sister's husband's sister's son, that is to say, a parallel relation to that which linked Pat with Séamus Murphy, but in this case the two men do not call themselves 'first cousins' – maybe because Willy also happens to be Pat's father's father's sister's daughter's son, i.e., his second cousin. Apart from these, Pat does not know the majority of people who are buying straw from him, since he got in touch with them through an advertisement in the local press.

Carrying bales of straw is not half as heavy as carrying bags of corn. A single man can load a full trailer without major problems. But it is always convenient for the straw buyers to have one or two helpers, just to make things faster, especially if they are buying a good few bales, which is why the majority of them came along with at least one relative or neighbour. Still, those who could not get enough help by themselves certainly appreciated any hand that could come from Pat's side. The two brothers from Mayo, for instance, got the help from Pat and myself most of the time they spent loading their lorry. But there were more people involved as well. Pat had sold a few bags of barley and oats to his neighbour James Connor and to two in-laws, one of his wife's brothers, Joe Naughton, and his wife's sister's husband, Brendan Glynn, the two of them very small farmers. They got a good bargain from Pat, which made them particularly vulnerable to the work demands of Pat's farm, and in this case, of Pat's straw buyers.

It strikes me that this brief transcription of an everyday social occasion shows very dramatically that even the most summary account of the most ordinary experience turns its theoretical distillation into a real nightmare for the writer of ethnography. It is a nightmare located in the irreducible complexity of all historical events, which seems to sterilise any attempt to make out their underlying principles so as to analyse them one by one, when in reality they nearly always appear all together and at the same time. But at this stage of my account I should put particular emphasis on the real complexity of the ethnographic images, because that complexity, or one aspect of that complexity, plays a constitutive role in the ensuing argument.

The reader will notice that this is a sort of 'liminal' chapter, half-way between the polar opposites or ideal types that articulate my narrative. Thus far we have been looking at one end of the spectrum: the 'contractual' type. I have defined what I call the contractual principle in terms of the anonymous and universalistic personality of the contracting parties and, closely related to this, in terms of the immediacy of the counter-services exchanged. It has been suggested that the application of such principle in its purest expression, that is to say, when the two characteristics I have just stated appear with utmost intensity, goes hand in hand with the 'moral' distance separating the parties.[1] This distance is at its maximum when dealing with strangers at the mart, or with the moral aliens of the itinerant bands, but much less clear when hiring a neighbour to bale one's hay, or giving a few pounds to his son when he comes to help out.[2] I was arguing then that in this latter case money acquires a symbolic value inversely correlated to its material relevance; it acquires the value to stand for a different type of social relationship nicely blended with the contractual link.

In all those cases, however, there was a reason for the maintenance of the contractual principle, if alongside other principles that sometimes seem to water it down. Now we have seen the operation of the same notion of immediate returns in the sphere of exchanges of farm products among farmers. Its justification is not to be found now in the idea of otherness that applies, with all due qualifications, to those who fall outside the farming community as moral community, be these stock dealers, itinerants, contractors, etc. But there is another sense in which

1. 'A contract, formal or informal, is regarded as a necessity in binding, for whatever purpose, parties who are not sufficiently united by other ties. To contract is to admit that other ties are lacking' (Freeman 1970: 197).
2. Similarly, Humphreys points out, referring to rural families, that whereas in their relations among themselves they tend to be particularistic, their dealings with outsider individuals tend to be universalistic (1966: 15). Cole and Wolf, on the other hand, observed that in the Alpine village of Tret the needs for extrafamily labour resources are met by the system of generalised reciprocity if they are obtained from within the boundaries of the village, balanced reciprocity if they come from a neighbouring village, and negative reciprocity if they are from a non-neighbouring village (1974: 168–71; cf. Sahlins 1972: 196–204; Gregory 1982: 42).

otherness comes into play in this type of exchanges. And this is precisely the fact that farmers are not looking for any additional relation of trust, originated in neighbourhood, kinship or whatever other source, when they sell or buy their farm produce. We will remember that many of the people who were buying straw from Pat got in touch with him through an advertisement in the local press; some of them came from as far as thirty miles away. Even though they all belonged to the farming community as an occupational category, many of them were absolute strangers in terms of any other relation that could link them with the other party. In these conditions, the anonymous and universalistic treatment sanctioned by a contractual relation, together with its requisite of immediate returns, looks very much like the most adequate form of engagement.

I therefore suggest that there are different kinds of otherness and, correspondingly, different kinds of 'moral communities'. A person can be 'other' in one sense and 'non-other' in another sense, and he or she can also be 'non-other' in more than one sense. In other words, if otherness appears to be related, with all due qualifications, to the application of the contractual principle, we see that the social function of such principle can be understood only on a situational basis, and only in the particular context in which it appears, a context that might confer upon the same legal form an entirely different social content.

But let me go back now to the commodity exchanges internal to the farming community (internal only in a relative sense). As has become quite apparent from the social scene that took place on the occasion both of Séamus Murphy's and Pat's harvests, the fact that neither of them was looking specifically for neighbours or relatives to buy their corn or straw does not mean that these will be necessarily absent from the stage. On the contrary, there is no reason why they should not figure prominently among the crowd of customers. Once again, the overlapping of the contractual link with other types of bonds might alter substantially its idiosyncratic principles. As one farmer put it to me, when you are selling a bag of corn to a neighbour or friend you will never ask to be paid on the spot, 'but this only happens with people you know well!' We remember Nocl Forde's experience when he trusted too much the man who bought a calf from him. By and large, what I said before about the payment of the services provided by neighbours should be repeated here.

But still there is another sense in which the stream of commodity exchanges springing from the corn harvest flows throughout the social structure of the community. The buying of corn or straw, especially in large quantities, requires the recruitment of a few helpers for loading the

trailers or lorries. And from this, the sphere of informal exchanges is con-
jured up to accomplish a task initially conceived as the actualisation of
the opposite principle. What at first perhaps began as an anonymous
contact through an advertisement in the local press, could very well end
up in the warm and friendly atmosphere of collective work at the corn
fields. We saw a similar instance in Chapter 4 when I defined the fairs
and the mart as platforms for the activation of the internal networks of
the farming community. To some extent it could be said that on that
occasion a new 'community' of reciprocal exchanges takes shape thanks
to the very process of commoditisation.[3] This is a community originated in the principle of restricted reciprocity in relation to the objects
but concluded by the principle of generalised reciprocity in relation to
the subjects. The unfolding of the spirit of contract seems to have turned
it into its antithesis.

The purpose of this chapter has been to show how the principle of
contract can be not only the principle of 'society' but also the principle
of 'community'. In what follows we will examine a set of social relations
that certainly appear, on the theoretical level, as the antithesis of the contractual principle. It could be argued, therefore, that my narrative follows the inverse order of the historical sequence postulated by Maine in
his well-known statement: 'we may say that the movement of the progressive societies has hitherto been a movement *from Status to Contract*'
([1864] 1986: 165). Going 'from Contract to Status' is not a way of
somehow calling into question Maine's evolutionist assumption. I would
rather justify my arrangement for analytical purposes, in terms of the
received wisdom of current social theory that leads anthropological
accounts from the known to the unknown, from the familiar to the less
familiar, from modernity to tradition, from capitalism to noncapitalism
or less capitalism.

3. It looks as if we were confronted by the inverse situation of that observed by
Malinowski in the Kula ring. There a ceremonial exchange that can be said to rein-
force some form of community bonds is used as a springboard for commercial
activities (1922: 83); here it is those commercial activities that seem to activate communitarian interaction.

8. Tönnies in the West of Ireland

*I*n some societies, there might be only a thin layer of contractual relations under which we would find a more substantive system of informal exchanges. In some others, that superficial layer appears to be much thicker, but still, it might be just a matter of digging a bit farther down in order to come across parallel systems of noncontractual transactions. And in many others, the two strata are so mixed that the distinction between formal and informal exchanges can be held only analytically.

The type of social relations we are going to see next constitutes a time-honoured object of study of social anthropologists. And they have been conceptualised in different terms and from different perspectives. Maine ([1864] 1986) placed the emphasis on the notion of *status* as opposed to that of contract; Tönnies ([1887] 1974) referred to *community* as the antithesis of what he called association or society; Mauss ([1950] 1990) elaborated the theory of *gift* exchanges in contrast to commodity exchanges (Gregory 1982); and, more lately, Sahlins (1972), borrowing from Lévi-Strauss, put forward the concept of *generalised reciprocity*, in opposition to both balanced and negative reciprocities. None of them is talking about exactly the same thing, but still there is some common ground on which all these theories seem to overlap. So far, we have seen that contractual regulations were being gradually twisted and distorted by the operation of a powerful social context, turning anonymity into personalism and immediate and determinate payment into delayed and indeterminate counter-services. It is the dialectics of these two principles that we should keep in mind in the forthcoming analysis.

In the west of Ireland, the word 'coor' somehow evokes that sphere of informal exchanges and of community ethos, but in a rather untidy fashion. The anglicised expression 'cooring', working 'in coor', is used by the people of the Three Districts when they talk about cooperation. It comes from the Irish word *comhar*, which at first referred simply to cotillage, but now has ended up meaning any type of alliance or partnership (Arensberg and Kimball [1940] 1968: 74–75). Two or more neighbours who usually help each other in their respective farms, two men who decide to share the ownership of a machine, or even just a group of people who have set up together any type of business, not necessarily related to the agricultural world, are all said to be in coor. But originally, the word coor had a more restrictive application.

To be or to work in coor with a man meant to exchange draught horses with him. As with many other agricultural machines such as the harrow and the hay mower, two horses are needed to draw a plough. Although practically every farmer would have more than one horse, it was very unusual for a farmer to have at one particular time two horses sufficiently well trained and well matched to draw a plough with the required accuracy. The swapping of horses between neighbours solved that problem.

Joseph Maloney and Joe Coady are two small full-time farmers who used to buy their horses together; one would keep the males and the other the females, and they also used to share the agricultural implements operated with them such as ploughs and harrows. Joseph, who is seventy-five years old, was already working in coor with Joe's father; and when Joe, who is now forty-five, took over the farm, he went on cooperating with the son. They are not next-door neighbours; their two farm houses are approximately one mile away from each other, although they have many adjacent fields. At any rate, the reason why they worked together, according to them, is that both were very fond of horses and they got along very well.

Declan, a part-time farmer, also remembers that his father exchanged horses and shared the plough with a neighbour, John Connor, for more than thirty years. He himself worked in coor with him too before getting his off-farm job; he says that he enjoyed every minute he worked with that man. When John's son took over he decided to sell the farm to a stranger – no more coor with this new resident. Whereas Joseph and Joe had more or less the same land, forty-five and fifty-four acres respectively, John Connor had almost twice as much as Declan. Differences in land holding were never an impediment for the swapping of horses; in fact, the more a horse was working in the fields, the better trained it would be. Differences in temperament and personal inclinations seem to account better for the cooring relationships.[1] We have seen that Declan never cooperated with his new neighbour when John's son got rid of the farm. Similarly, Joseph Maloney's son, who is currently running the farm, and Joe Coady do not seem to share too many things. There are no horses around any more; maybe Joseph's son could not find any other reason to justify the keeping of a cooperative relation with Joe than his outdated experience with horses.

In any case, what is undeniable at the moment is that the work with horses has disappeared altogether from the Irish rural landscape, and from this the ploughing of the fields has certainly lost its social scene. Still, although tractors are not swapped as horses were, most farmers do not mind loaning their ploughs and harrows; they are not particularly delicate items of machinery, so practically anyone can use them without major risks for the owner – maybe an indication that old patterns of sociability always die hard.

When you ask country people about work in cooperation they invariably say that this has changed an awful lot, that there was much more cooperation in years gone by. 'Neighbours would be always helping each other,' an old bachelor told me. 'When you finished your work if your neighbour was still at it you would jump the wall and give him a hand … Now everybody keeps for himself, I don't know the hell why … Aye, it was a crack to go and help … and money was never involved, you see (they had no money at that time), just help.' 'There was plenty of people around,' pointed out Tomás Reegan. 'Now people have emigrated, but in those days, there was plenty of lads available, and you would not pay those who helped you, they were fed and they might get a couple of bob, that's all. Nobody would do anything for that now.' 'In the old times, you would be ploughing with the horses', said another bachelor, 'and someone would come along with the bike, and you would stop for a few minutes, have a fag, and maybe he would give you a hand afterwards, that kind of thing.' Jimmy Doherty remembered that in those days you would stay at a neighbour's house until very late at night, and the following morning you would go working together. All that is gone now. It is all because people don't visit any more, he argued, now that they have cars, they travel.

---

1. A farmer from Co. Fermanagh is said to have claimed that 'you never know a man until you plough with him' (O'Dowd 1981: 121).

Most of these men were only small children when Arensberg and Kimball did their seminal fieldwork; some of them were not even born. But curiously enough, the two American anthropologists met with answers very similar to those I have just reported. 'The need of the small farmer for his fellows is no longer so great. Monetary hire is spreading into the country communities' ([1940] 1968: 264). Even though they remarked that the foundation of mutual relations upon which reciprocal help was based still existed, the old people denied that there was any community effort at that time (p. 268). It becomes a slippery question to find out what historical period my Irish friends refer to when they talk about 'the old days'. It could well be that the work in cooperation has been in decline for a very long time. But in any case, it is certainly striking to realise that more than fifty years ago one would come across the same tendency to portray a none-too-distant past as a paradise of communitarian interaction, and the same tendency to misrecognise or downplay the current version of reciprocal aid.

There is the widespread idea that the so-called modernisation of rural societies goes hand in hand with increased individualisation of the productive processes and social life in general terms. As a matter of fact, my informants' opinions about the demise of cooperation deeply reverberate throughout much of the literature on peasant and post-peasant societies. Erasmus (1956), for instance, argued in his classic study on the disappearance of reciprocal farm labour that technological progress and its concomitant development of the division of labour makes reciprocal exchanges rather difficult, because those exchanges are based on equal qualities of labour. This argument has been supported in Ireland by Hannan's initial research on social change in Irish rural communities (1972), from which he concluded that:

> The tractor technology was so qualitatively different from the horse-based one that it was very difficult to integrate it into the mutually understood and reciprocally balanced system of equivalent exchanges of labour and horse-power ... These initial difficulties in working out the new terms of trade were compounded by the new cultural differences then arising, when interests in personal gain and individual family advancement were replacing the more communal orientation of earlier times (Hannan 1972: 180–81; cf. Brody 1973: 131–56).[2]

2. However, he also pointed out that the disintegrating mutual aid system 'has been replaced by a confusing series of local dyadic or triadic alliances amongst the more commercialised farmers; and in many cases, given the newly increased case of intercommunication, by the strengthening of the local but more widely scattered kin group' (Hannan 1972: 182).

The erosion of cooperative institutions by technological development has its logical counterpart in technological stagnation wherever it is the case that those cooperative institutions have persisted. That is the reason why such persistence has been held responsible for the general underdevelopment of the Irish economy (Hutchinson 1970: 522–23; cf. Breen 1981: 153–54). Whatever is the truth of this argument, it seems to rest on the assumption that technological development sprouts from competition, so that cooperative attitudes will necessarily hinder that development. In reality, however, this postulate is far from conclusive.

Erasmus's initial theories have been seriously questioned by later ethnographies, such as Brandes's study of a Castilian village. Brandes has consistently demonstrated that, even though it is true that economic development gives rise to the development of the division of labour, it takes place at the level of the whole society and not of the local community. Consequently, the general process of the division of labour could very well end up in a specialisation of the local community and, therefore, in an increased homogenisation of its productive units, which in turn would foster stronger communitarian feelings (Brandes 1975: 75–77 and 102–5).

On the other hand, the correlation of economic rationality and profit-maximising attitudes with asocial and anticooperative behaviour does not seem to have been fully borne out by the facts. In his analysis of the Irish entrepreneur's mentality, Brody observed that 'the new entrepreneurial family finds no difficulty – symbolic, emotional or material – in co-operating with relatives in advancing their economic interest' (1973: 202), and also that 'refusal to join with others in pursuit of economic improvements is an important element in the overall trends towards the isolation of households and reduced interest in farming itself' (p. 201).[3] Similarly, Hannan himself qualified his arguments in a later work, where he pointed out that:

> Those who have successfully modernised have not done so through a socially destructive and aggressive individualism. Indeed all the evidence suggests the opposite. It is the successful who have maintained the strongest ties with kin and neighbour groups. The most isolated and most alienated from kin and neighbour groups are found amongst those who have not adapted successfully – declassed, without heirs

---

3. The reason why the crofters of the Shetland islands do not cooperate is, according to Cohen, that 'co-operation *could* make crofting economically viable. But that would be to apply an entirely inappropriate philosophy to people's view of crofting' (1987: 100–101).

and, of all groups, least likely to have strong kinship or neighbour group bonds. Economic marginalisation has had very destructive consequences on social bonds (1979: 19; see also Hannan and Katsiaouni 1977: 171–72).

If it is true therefore that economic rationality does not have to be necessarily at odds with cooperation, this also undermines another widespread prejudice as to the essential 'moral basis' of cooperative attitudes.[4] Many studies of farming communities have questioned the early postulate that such attitudes sprang from a sort of blind obedience to a moral rule, from a communitarian ethos gradually eroded by the introduction of the individualist economic rationality of capitalist culture. On the contrary, cooperative behaviour is understood now as a result of the cooperators' craving for maximising their material profits. 'It is not the moral obligations of membership, but specific interests of the people, that determine the composition of permanent working groups', Iturra observed among Galician farmers (1977: 82). Similarly, Abrahams has pointed out that, for his Finnish friends, 'co-operation should be seen as an act of will, arising from the exercise of choice and, thus, enhancing rather than detracting from the individual identity of those involved' (1991: 145). Bailey has gone so far as to assert that it is precisely the 'destruction of community life' that enhances cooperation, and not the other way round:

> The diversification of ways of making a living, which comes about through incorporation into a larger economy, automatically cuts down the frequency of exchanges, restricts the flow of information, and so increases ignorance about one's neighbour and thus promotes that paradoxical ignorance and indifference which decreases jealousy and opens the way towards various kinds of co-operation (Bailey 1971: 298; cf. Hanssen 1979/80: 112–13).

We have already seen in Brandes's study that such incorporation into the larger economy does not always give rise to what Bailey seems to take as the premise for his reasoning: the diversification of ways of living at the local level. In any case, as for my own fieldwork experience, it did not

---

4. In his well-known study of the Italian peasantry, Banfield pointed out that the ideology of amoral familism prevented the Montegranesi from cooperation and, therefore, blocked economic development. Nevertheless, to substitute 'altruism' for amoral familism was not the solution. Banfield maintained that amoral familism, devoid of its most negative aspects, could also be appropriate for economic development to the extent that it was predicated upon an individualistic, self-interested ethos (Banfield 1958: 165–67).

seem to me that interhousehold cooperation could be understood, too explicitly to say the least, in terms of strict economic rationality or profit-maximising attitudes. Far from that, 'moral' arguments such as 'we help each other because we are good neighbours', or 'good friends', etc., come out quite frequently. I would say that we are confronted by an instance similar to what we encountered in Chapter 6, when we were discussing the moral wrapping of the relations between farmers and contractors. On the other hand, as I argued there, I do not see why economic development, or economic rationality, has necessarily to be hindered by the justification of a particular behaviour in moral terms.[5]

I would suggest that an important theoretical distinction be emphasised if we want to make a better sense of the culture of cooperation in farming communities. We will see it through a particular example. We know so far that a certain affinity between modernisation and individualism has been traditionally postulated. I would say that in the Three Districts there is a particular type of farming, the dairy business, that embodies people's perceptions of modernisation; and again, to a certain degree, the antisocial ghost of individualism seems to haunt the spirit of modernity in this particular case.

The work of a dairy farmer is qualitatively different from that of his dry-stock colleagues. He is submitted to the direst strictures in the implementation of his tasks and, to some extent as a result of it, his labour process appears to be extremely individualised. Milking is a solitary task that has to be performed twice a day with the strictest regularity. The help of a willing wife is always welcomed, but it will hardly alleviate the work demands involved unless it is she who does the whole milking. Furthermore, it should be taken into account, as Bouquet has observed among Devon farmers (1985), that the mechanisation of the milking process and, above all, the specialisation of dairy enterprises, have brought about the masculinisation of a task that not long ago figured prominently among women's exclusive prerogatives.[6]

It could be argued that the austere individualisation of the productive process in the case of the dairy farmer is somehow compensated for by a strong drive toward associationism as far as the process of milk distribution is concerned. There are two things to be considered when we look

---

5. And what is 'economic development', anyhow? After the latest CAP reforms (drastic reduction of surpluses), I do not think that there is an easy answer to that question.

6. 'A woman's smaller hands make it "natural" for her to be a better hand at milking the cows' (Arensberg and Kimball [1940] 1968: 49).

at the commercialisation of milk. First, there is the system of quotas established by the EC in 1983. Each dairy farmer is allocated a quota of milk production, which cannot be exceeded, in such a way that all dairy farmers who produce according to their quota can be absolutely sure that their milk will be sold, even though they never know at what price. Second, quotas have a creamery cooperative assigned, which is obliged to buy the entire milk production of the dairy farmers owning those quotas and who have produced according to them. Every second day the truck of the cooperative goes from farm to farm collecting the milk, and every month farmers receive their cheque for the milk they have been supplying. This quota system makes the dairy farmer seem like a privileged producer to his dry-stock colleagues, who can realise the value of their production maybe only once or twice a year, and, for that reason, they are at a clear disadvantage in the face of the fluctuations of the market; this is apart from the fact that they are not protected against the dangers of over-production by any system of quotas.

It is worth describing briefly the nature of milk cooperatives, since it will help us gain some insights into this intricate question of cooperation in farming communities in terms of the dichotomy between production and distribution. The cooperative movement in Ireland started in the 1890s, and at present creamery cooperatives have practically monopolised the commercialisation of milk and dairy products and, to some extent, the commercialisation of dry stock (see Chapter 4).[7] The capital of the cooperative is distributed among small shareholders, who individually might have up to a thousand pounds. These are the dairy farmers themselves or the so-called 'dry shareholders', people who are not in the dairy business any more but who still keep some shares. The purpose of these shares is 'to have something owned by all the farmers', rather than to earn any dividends, since all profits are reinvested on a regular basis. But as shareholders do not necessarily have to be milk producers, in the same way the latter do not have to be shareholders either. The profits of the cooperative, on the other hand, come from all sorts of different sources. Apart from those stemming directly from the commercialisation of milk, the cooperative owns the livestock mart and several farm shops; the sale and purchase of milk quotas have to be done through the cooperative, and it also functions as a credit institution.

It should be clear from even the most superficial enquiry into the running of the creamery cooperative that in no way can it be seen as an

---

7. For a detailed analysis of cooperatives in the west of Ireland, see Curtin and Varley (1989).

alternative to capitalism from the point of view of its internal logic. The creamery cooperative operates according to the principle of profit, the same as any other capitalist business. This principle stems not so much from the private selfishness of an isolating individualist ethos, as a naive vision of capitalist culture would tend to suggest, but from the objective imperatives of the free-market economy, wherein the cooperative has to realise the value of its commodities. The control exercised by the cream-ery cooperative over the commercialisation of milk can be said to have superseded the blind competition at the level of milk producers only to restore it at the level of the relations existing between creameries them-selves, whether cooperatives or individually owned businesses – although free competition is certainly distorted at all levels by the system of quotas.

But the point I wish to make here is this: even making allowances for such overcoming of individualist attitudes among milk producers by the institution of cooperatives,[8] this transcendence of individualism *at the level of distribution* turns out to be qualitatively different from the tran-scendence of individualism that exists *at the level of production*. In one sense, individualism is transcended by means of the very devices sup-plied by capitalist culture: associationism. But in the other sense, there is an important discontinuity with the cultural system of capitalism. That is why the opposition production/distribution turns out to be not simply the opposition between two different economic moments of the same social whole, but between two different social universes articulated in the same economic process.

The opposition between production and distribution in the west of Ireland is somehow evocative of Tönnies's dichotomy between commu-nity and association ([1887] 1974). Unlike what occurs in the sphere of distribution, to a great extent under the control of the cooperative move-ment, I found very little 'associative' mood among the farmers of the Three Districts with regard to the implementation of their productive processes.[9] This lack of associationism does not mean that the 'spirit of

8. This should in fact be further qualified to the extent that not all milk producers receive the same price per gallon. The cooperative has established three different prices according to the quality of the milk supplied (concentration of bacteria). But this affects the price paid to the milk supplier and not the price of the final dairy product that the creamery will commercialise in the free market. So it could be said that the creamery makes extra profits at the expense of the suppliers of low-quality milk. And in this sense, it encourages some degree of competition among the suppliers so as to improve the quality of their milk.

9. This is in sharp contrast with much of my data on the Catalan stockbreeders of the plains. The most extreme case of associative activity referring to the process of production was

contract' is completely absent from the sphere of production; it simply means that the penetration of contractualism into that sphere has not given rise to the proliferation of any type of *ad hoc* associations. Cooperation in the process of production, therefore, does not take place on the basis of associative principles, but on the basis of an entirely different ethos that, for lack of a better expression, I will define with Tönnies's concept of community.

Whereas in an association we might argue that the individual appears as a condition of possibility of the whole, in a community it is the whole that becomes the condition of possibility of the individual. A contract can be seen only as the result of the contracting wills, which appear as its logical antecedent. Two neighbours, in contrast, can be seen only as the product of a preexisting neighbourhood, which similarly appears as their logical antecedent. This point will be more clear after a careful study of the particular contexts that I claim are defined by this community ethos.[10]

---

that of five small dairy farmers who decided to join their respective herds and set up a collective milking parlour. Even though, as far as I could observe, this was rather an unusual arrangement, 'associative feelings' among these Catalan farmers seem to be quite widespread, but only in the sphere of production. In the sphere of distribution, in contrast, and somewhat paradoxically, the cooperative movement in Catalonia lags far behind its Irish counterpart.

10. There is a nice 'discrepancy' of this definitely classical form of reasoning and current anthropological theories of Maussian inspiration, according to which commodity exchanges are predicated on a preexisting sociopolitical order as gift exchanges are understood as creating the sociopolitical order (Sahlins 1972: 168–72; Hart 1986). The discrepancy is more apparent than real. A gift creates a social relationship if it is taken in isolation but not if considered as a counter-gift for a previous service, in which case it appears as the fulfilment of a preexisting debt. But to see a gift as a some sort of payment goes against 'the spirit of the gift'!

9. The Intricacies of the Gift

*L*et me go back to the cooring relations that I introduced at the begin-ning of the previous chapter. There are no records in Ireland of formally institutionalised patterns of cooperative work similar to those found in other parts of Europe,[1] and yet work in cooperation has a long tradition in Irish rural society. I would dare to say that it has been precisely this lack of corporate organisation that has conferred upon the Irish culture of reciprocal aid its distinctive character. It is interesting to point out, on the other hand, that the notion of cooperation as resulting from sponta-neous help, and not from the stipulations of a customary or legal rule, encapsulates a certain folk concept of ethnic identity, of specificity of the Irish national character, maybe in opposition to its traditional enemy, the individualist Anglo-Saxon world.

Commenting on the establishment of the water scheme, the organi-sation that has promoted the building of a current water network in the rural areas of Co. Galway, a contributor to the local press made the fol-lowing observation:

> [a marvellous facet] about the group water scheme was the fact that it was a superb example of the 'self-help' spirit that so typifies much of our tradition, the tradition of 'meitheal' [working party]. In the case

---

1. Cf. Ott (1981) for the Basque Pyrenees. The most comprehensive study of traditional patterns of cooperation in rural Ireland has been done by the folklorist Anne O'Dowd (1981), who has compiled up to thirty-eight different names for cooperative practices documented in the archives of the Irish Folklore Commission.

of the group schemes, families came together in their hundreds to put up money and sometimes to dig the very foundations themselves for the pipes carrying the water (*Connacht Tribune*, 13 July 1990).

Even more explicit was Noel Forde in talking about relations of good neighbourliness. He asserted proudly that if he ever ran into trouble, all the neighbours would tell each other and everybody would help him immediately; 'This is very Irish', he emphasised. And then he went on referring to a friend of his who had emigrated to America; whenever he needed assistance from his neighbours, he had to pay for it, whereas he had offered to help out for no pay. Again: 'He was an Irishman!'

He was an Irishman, one could argue, brought up in what certainly constitutes an ancient form of social solidarity preserved in the rural communities of the west of Ireland, in the cradle of the 'Gaelic way of life', where so many things have been kept safe from the ravages of modern civilisation. When I asked a middle-aged farmer whether he had ever worked for other farmers, he denied it straightaway. 'Not for pay, anyhow', he added. Have you worked for no pay, then? 'Well, that's the way it is here, you see; you are with them and they are with you, that kind of thing', he replied. 'We work in coor here, we help each other,' an old bachelor tells me. 'Whenever I am stuck I just call on a neighbour and he will help me. The farmer has no timetable, you see, nothing happens if I spend a few hours with a neighbour.'

In dealing with 'community' patterns of cooperative work, the first thing we have to take into account is that they never, or very rarely, appear as a separate sphere, rigidly segregated from other forms of labour relationships. On the contrary, as has already been suggested, generalised reciprocity, work exchanges, nonmonetary transactions of any type, all seem to mix well with the more formalised contractual bonds that we studied before. The point I would like to stress here is that the conditions of possibility of such varied combinations of social bonds stem to a great extent from the flexible nature of the labour process itself – 'anyone would do'. It is important to underline this notion of flexibility, because this is a characteristic to be found in many farm jobs. There is a remarkable correlation between flexibility of the labour process and the proliferation of informal patterns of cooperation, even though the sense in which these two circumstances appear associated would require a closer examination. We could argue that the softness of the technical constraint enables the farmer to play out his network of social relationships to better suit his interests.

The combination between formal and informal social bonds on the one hand and, on the other, the importance of the constraints stemming from the characteristics of the labour process itself can both be taken as the 'external' factors that contribute to the definition of informal cooperation as a working relationship. Let us have a look now at what we could define as the internal structure of such relationship.

This internal structure could be described in terms of three types of oppositions. The first opposition refers to the rules that regulate the different ways in which a particular type of help is reciprocated. Thus far I have been making the distinction between immediate returns and delayed returns to discriminate between what I call contractual relations and relations of generalised reciprocity, between formal and informal models of interaction, between monetary and nonmonetary exchanges. But within this second field of informal relations, a further division should be entered. On the one hand, we have those situations wherein everybody seems to be working for everybody else at the same time (for example, dipping or shearing sheep), or, similarly, those situations in which, even though there is not collective work for collective ends, there is a certain notion of a *quid pro quo* or *do ut facias* that certainly brings us near to the spirit of contract.[2] On the other hand, there are other occasions when such feeling of immediate returns, of quasi-contract, is entirely absent: the casual help given by a neighbour who passes by on his bike.

The second opposition has to do with the object of the relations of informal cooperation, in particular, the opposition between work and machinery. Finally, the third opposition refers to the subjects involved, as it seems that those who participate in those relationships invariably fall into two categories: they are either neighbours or kinsmen. I will return to this later on. But now let me highlight another important aspect of the culture of informal labour relationships.

It should be noted that both work exchanges and machinery loans circulate within specific networks of reciprocal aid, and patterns of interaction and sociability are developed from such networks. Similarly to what Anthony Cohen has pointed out as regards kinship, that it is defined not just as a 'morphology of social relations', but also as a 'rhetoric of legitimation' (1987: 66), we could argue that the language of farm work, with reference to the implementation of tasks and to the use of farm equipment, expresses in this sense not only the *technical* side of

---

2. The concept of barter should be included here (see Humphrey and Hugh-Jones 1992).

the labour process, but also, and more importantly, its *social* constitution. Very often people talk about how delicate certain machines are, to justify their wish not to let anyone have borrowing rights over them, or to lend them only to very particular individuals. In the same way, they will claim that they never cooperate with so-and-so, or they never ask him for help when they are stuck, because he is too busy, too old, he does not have the right tools, he is careless, etc. In such a way their choice very often appears as the most adequate from the technical point of view. In other words, the sociability of work is recurrently represented in terms of technical efficiency.

I do not presuppose that the language of farm work constitutes a mere subterfuge for the constitution of social bonds, a crafty ideology conceived so as to disguise under the harmless imperatives of technical necessities one's less innocent or more embarrassing personal commitments and affections. I am simply suggesting that what from one point of view appears as a cluster of social engagements, from another point of view is seen as the mere execution of a set of farm jobs, and that both levels of reality, so to speak, find their expression in the same idiom, the language of farm work, but none of them is more or less 'true' than the other.

Another of Gudeman's 'metaphors of livelihood' (1986) seems to be involved here. But in this case, it is not a social rhetoric that is used to talk about economic life, but somehow the other way around: an economic jargon further simplified to its barest technological core appears as a metaphor for the social order. As any ethnographer can corroborate, to talk about social relations is not always an easy task, and if this can be done through the mediation of an innocuous technical language, so much the better – especially when those social relations entail certain inequalities and imbalances very likely to evoke uncomfortable hierarchies.

I have already said that manual work and machinery loans are mutually exchangeable, and if it could be argued that *a priori* everybody has the same working potential, that is certainly not the case as far as machinery ownership is concerned.[3] Even though this is a rule overshadowed by so many exceptions, the bigger the farmer the more likely he is to have good equipment in abundance, and vice versa, the smaller the farmer the less profitable for him to have too many machines if they

3. 'Large farms are better equipped than others and their smaller neighbours depend on them a great deal. On the other hand, the large farm requires additional labour on many occasions, and in borrowing its machines the little farmer incurs the obligation to give a day's work now and again in exchange' (Rees 1950: 93).

are only for his own use – if he plans to go on hire with them, that is a different matter altogether. But on the other hand, as Alwyn Rees accurately observed in his Welsh community, the big farmers are more vulnerable to labour deficits than their smaller colleagues who, conversely, might very well find themselves in an excess of labour supply.

Such is the situation of Jimmy Doherty and his neighbour Denis Jordan. Jimmy is a middle-aged bachelor who lives with his elderly parents on twenty-five acres of land. Denis is married to a good working wife, but his four children are still too small to be of any use on the farm, and to work his seventy-nine acres he more than often needs the help of another adult man. With such a tiny farm, Jimmy never thought it worth buying any machine, not even a tractor, but he always has some of Denis's farm utensils around the house. In exchange, he is always ready to offer his help when needed, carrying bags of corn, picking potatoes, putting in bales of hay, things like that. Before working for Denis, Jimmy used to help out two bachelor brothers who lived down the road, but one of them died and the other one sold the farm and moved away, and he has been with Denis ever since.

The same relationship can be seen between Noel Forde (120 acres) and his first cousin John Casey (40 acres). John often does bits and pieces on his kinsman's farm, and in exchange he seems to be entitled to borrow whatever he needs. Once I saw John working a full day for Noel, collecting bales of hay. Noel wanted to pay him twenty pounds but he did not accept. He told me later that his two sons had worked for Noel too when they were young. On the other hand, it is not only kinship that links John and Noel's families: their two wives happen to be very good friends. In fact, Noel's wife was the bridesmaid at John's wedding, and that is how Noel met her for the first time.

Before going a little farther into the subject of inequalities in reciprocal exchanges, let me provide the reader with some of the 'flavour' of cooperative work as I experienced it myself working for Pat Sheridan, since this turns out to be particularly relevant to the question at issue. With 180 acres of arable land, Pat also happens to be the biggest farmer of the parish. He is a man with a very good reputation in the community. Despite the fact that he has more than three times the average land ownership, and that so many of his neighbours have been working for him at some stage, I could never detect any feeling of envy or bitterness toward him. On the contrary, many people would pity him for the large amount of work he has to do in looking after such a huge farm, and they would boast of being able to keep going with much less. I recorded up to ten different people who could somehow be included in Pat's network of cooperators, nicely divided into two categories: five relatives and five neighbours.

On one occasion Pat wanted to store his recently bought combine harvester in a neighbour's shed. Since the shed was full of rotten hay, he decided to ask Jim O'Brien for help to clean it. Jim is an old bachelor who lives with his sister and a mentally handicapped brother on a twenty-eight-acre farm, not too far from the shed Pat wanted to use. Jim also happens to be the owner's mother's brother. 'Ah!, there is no work there,' he said when we went to ask him. 'The only thing you'll have to do is to look at the road and move your head when somebody passes by!' So eventually he decided to send his brother to give us a hand, and he spent most of the time messing around with a fork and not fully committed to doing any real work. A few days later, we were going to the farm with a trailer full of turf when we met him again on the road. He agreed with Pat to come along the following day to put in that turf. 'I'll give him a few pounds; he might be more willing to help then', Pat commented to me. But days passed and the man did not turn up. The one who eventually came was Jim himself, not to put in the turf but to ask Pat whether he could weld a platform for the battery of his old tractor. Pat spent more than four hours trying to weld the piece. When he finally finished it, Jim left, not before having taken his cup of tea in the house. In the end, Pat decided to put in the turf himself.

Working with Pat, I learnt that for him and for the people of the Three Districts the work of a farm is much more than a mere economic practice, even though its economic significance confers upon it its distinctive character as regards other social activities. Whenever we went to somebody else's farm to ask for some implement or to collect something that had been borrowed before, we would spend a good while there helping out with whatever task was being done at that moment, and only later would we make explicit the purpose of our visit. Work does not lose its economic significance because of that courtesy, but it becomes at the same time a very fundamental act of social recognition among the members of the farming community. It is an expression of their social solidarity as an occupational category, since, quite obviously, only those who are in the same job can express their social solidarity through work exchanges.

I pointed out at the beginning of this chapter that on many occasions those work exchanges involved relatively homogeneous labour, so that a certain notion of *quid pro quo* could be grasped, no matter how vaguely.

But I also stressed that on many other instances the services exchanged become too heterogeneous to be measured by the same yardstick, especially when the use of machinery was also involved. Eventually, we encountered a situation in which even the very notion of equivalence would seem almost contradictory to the spirit of disinterested help.[4] As a matter of fact, people would never talk to me about work exchanges in terms of any type of correspondence between what is given and what is received; even when they were able to point to some sort of counter-service for the former help, it seems to me that it was more out of my own insistence on asking them about what they do or what they get in exchange than out of a really spontaneous definition of the relationship in those terms.[5]

People seem to pay much less attention to what is exchanged than to whom is actually engaged in such exchange. This is nothing new; it is a corollary of the spirit of mutual aid, well documented in the same terms as I have done by the majority of ethnographers who have done fieldwork in the west of Ireland.[6] Moreover, unlike what so many people in this part of the country tend to assume, this is not a peculiar characteristic of Irish rural communities. It has also been observed in many other parts of Europe and elsewhere, and sometimes not too far from the Irish scene. Among Welsh farmers, for instance, Rees pointed out with his customary insight that

---

4. Cf. Malinowski's classification of gifts, payments and commercial transactions among the Trobriands (1922: 177–91) of which he observed that 'although there exist forms of barter pure and simple, there are so many transitions and gradations between that and simple gift, that it is impossible to draw any fixed line between trade on the one hand, and exchange of gifts on the other' (p. 176).

5. 'When informants are asked, "If you help Fulano to collect hay, will he help you later on?" they invariably reveal a reluctance to answer the question directly. People become uncomfortable at the implication of forced assistance and, after hedging a few moments, state, "Perhaps", or "Not necessarily, but maybe"' (Brandes 1975: 84; cf. Arensberg and Kimball 1965: 122–23; Mewett 1982: 112).

6. Brody (1973: 131 56) has done to my knowledge one of the most thoughtful studies of the cooring relations, despite the fact that he was actually more interested in the demise of community structures than in their functional logic and, as a result of it, he had to base his analysis on his informants' accounts and not on his direct participant observation (cf. Arensberg and Kimball [1940] 1968: 74–75). It is a pity that so many good anthropologists working in the west of Ireland and elsewhere in Europe have been so naively haunted by the 'crave for the primitive', not realising that some of the institutions they recorded as already extinguished in their ghost villages could still be seen thriving in more 'modernised' communities.

There is no formal contract, neither is there an exact measurement of benefits conferred as against benefits received. Such calculations would be alien to the spirit of friendliness which pervades the whole system. After all, you cannot fully repay a neighbour who has helped you to harvest a crop under threatening clouds until you find him in similar difficulties (Rees 1950: 93; cf. Williams 1956: 152).

The definition of generalised reciprocity seems to partake in a socially recognised unawareness of the terms of exchange, an unawareness, on the other hand, that appears as a functional requisite dictated by the specific nature of the services in circulation.

Pitt-Rivers made a very similar point in his analysis of friendship relations in an Andalusian village. 'People assure one another that the favour they do is done with no afterthought,' he observed, 'a pure favour which entails no obligation, an action which is done for the pleasure of doing it, prompted only by the desire to express esteem' (1971: 138). But the paradox, then, is that 'while a friend is entitled to expect a return of his feeling and favour he is not entitled to bestow them in that expectation' (p. 139). It is the very logic of the relationship itself, therefore, on the basis of the incommensurability of its object, that abrogates the notion of equivalence. As Bourdieu has argued, 'gift exchange is one of the social games that cannot be played unless the players refuse to acknowledge the objective truth of the game' (1990: 105).

Still, it could be argued that a certain objective balance has to be achieved sooner or later; a certain rate of exchange, even if subjectively ignored, has to become objectively apparent in the long run. Similarly to what we were discussing in the case of the language of farm work, one would be tempted to see in that socially constructed ignorance another ideological artifice to shield the impertinence of a latent inequality. This artifice is what many anthropologists have denounced in their analysis of 'communitarian' social relationships. 'Almost never is an even balance in reciprocal labor struck between any two individuals', Brandes remarked of his Castilian farmers, since 'people with few animals, hence little hay, assist more than they are assisted' (1975: 85). And the same conclusion was reached by B.J. O'Neill concerning his Portuguese peasants: 'Reciprocal exchanges of labour at threshing function in the long run economically in favour of wealthier households at the expense of poorer households' labour'. 'This is not a conscious exploitation of labour on the part of the wealthier households,' he pointed out, 'but rather a form of inequality masked by an ideology of equality' (O'Neill 1987: 172).

I once asked one of my neighbours if he did not consider it unfair that a man who wants to have his hay baled on a reciprocal basis has to give his manual labour in exchange. While one is comfortably sitting on the baler, the other is sweating blood carrying bales; should he not receive further compensation for his strenuous work? But my neighbour did not seem to grasp my point. On the contrary, he argued, it is rather the one who is offering manual labour who should give a few pounds to the owner of the baler and not the other way around, because the one who drives the machine undoubtedly has more expenses than the other.[7] The old trick again, I thought: the owner of capital, or 'dead labour', as Marx put it, has the right to appropriate the live labour of his less fortunate colleagues. And if there is any surplus, it would go to the one with better bargaining power, who more than likely will be the machinery owner, to the extent that he can haggle with a more scarce resource than labour force. At the end of the day, the very simple law of supply and demand appears as the almighty rule that regulates reciprocal exchanges, in the same way as it regulates the exchange of commodities in the rest of the economy.

Therefore, the one who holds sway over more (scarce) resources, machinery in this case, is the one who will dictate the terms of equivalence. This was in essence Peter Gibbon's argument (1973) in his critique of both Arensberg and Kimball's and Brody's accounts of cooring relationships. For him, they all participate in an idealisation of traditional Irish rural communities; the fact that the American anthropologists stressed functional regularities, whereas Brody put forward a more dynamic, historically informed image, does not make any difference to Gibbon. They all failed to notice that the introduction of machinery into the system of reciprocal labour exchanges had long distorted their time-honoured egalitarianism, and logically to the advantage of those few who could appropriate that machinery.

There is no doubt that, in any exchange relation, the party who controls more or more scarce resources enjoys a privileged position. It does not matter whether this exchange is done under a system of delayed and indeterminate returns or whether it is a simple monetary transaction. The problem with Gibbon's thesis, as Rosemary Harris has rightly pointed out (1988), is that he takes farm machinery as the only resource

7. Thomas and Znaniecki maintained that to reciprocate borrowings according to the sacrifice of the owner and not in relation to the benefits obtained by the borrower was the result of the weakening of social solidarity and the development of 'economic attitudes' among the peasantry (Thomas and Znaniecki [1918–20] 1984: 83–86).

to be exchanged for labour force. In those conditions, it is obvious that the one who owns machinery can certainly appropriate the labour of his less capitalised neighbour. But relations of exchange in a farming community are slightly more complex than in a market economy. Machinery, important as it is, does not seem to be the only resource available. 'Detailed data on resources', Harris asserts, 'show the importance of recognising that power is unequal and the way in which it relates to the control of resources. However, they reveal the plural nature of these resources and their essentially "untidy" distribution in class terms' (1988: 433).

And so we approach the intricate question of finding out what actually circulates in the networks of exchange of a farming community, apart from work and machinery. In this, the people of the Three Districts fully demonstrate the characteristic that Abrahams has detected among his Finnish farmers: 'Informal patterns of collaboration and reciprocity are in fact best seen as part of the more general fabric of interaction between villagers. Help with some task on the farm does not seem to be distinguished sharply by the people from help in other contexts, though there are some pressures towards it' (Abrahams 1991: 158–59).

What other contexts? It has been suggested that people take more notice of who is exchanging things with them than about what is being exchanged. This matches the notion of personalism, so widespread in rural areas of Europe and particularly in Ireland. But why is that so important? What makes a noncontractual transaction possible is that it takes place within the normative framework provided by a wider social space. This is also what differentiates this type of exchange from contractual agreements, which have been traditionally defined as purely 'economic' arrangements devoid of any sort of 'social' interference. In the following chapters I will try to show the characteristics of the social spaces that provide the farm economy with its social character, and we will think about the reasons why those social spaces enable the development of a sphere of informal transactions in the farm economy.

10. FAMILY AND GENDER

The first of the social spaces we are going to examine is the farming family. In a rural community such as that of the Three Districts, the family and its farm constitute the most fundamental institutions. Between the family farm and the farming community we can envisage a homologous relationship to that between the ego and his kindred in an ego-centred kinship system,[1] 'where people operate independently, but need on occasion to call in help for some purposes' (Fox 1967: 166). This structural parallelism reminds us somehow of the fundamental contradiction of any social formation based on a family farm economy, that between the two domains that intersect at the family farm itself. On the one hand, there is the family, which encapsulates notions of the private, the domestic, the particular, the 'social' and, of course, the female, the reproductive sphere, the emotional. On the other hand there is the farm, which seems to conjure up ideas about the public, the universal, the economic, and thus, the masculine, the productive sphere, the rational.

As Abrahams has underscored, families are dynamic groups with their own developmental processes and inner conflicts, 'and they by no means automatically fit well with the demands of farming' (1991: 72). The structure of a family farm appears to be the result of an uneasy compromise between its two constitutive principles. I began talking about the farm economy of the Three Districts from, if I may use this expression,

---

1. 'The farms are not outlying members of a nucleated community, but entities in themselves, and their integration into social groups depends upon the direct relationships between them rather than upon their convergence on a single centre' (Rees 1950: 100).

its 'economic' side, from the market itself, the arena of the anonymous and universalistic *par excellence*. But gradually, we have seen how the 'noneconomic' was permeating the sharp ends of our materialistic picture. It is time now to shift our attention to the source of that noneconomic contamination; it is time to go from the family farm to the farming family.

Taking into account an absolutely dominant mode of land acquisition through patrilineal impartible inheritance, out of the 65 families of my sample, 14 can be seen as stem families in the following sense: they all had at least one surviving member of the previous land-owning generation living in the same house as the nuclear family of the farm manager. Of the remaining 51, 22 had had the old couple in the same house at some stage, but they were dead when I did the interview; 9 had the old couple still alive but living in the old house, while the farm manager's nuclear family was usually in a newly built bungalow only a few yards from the old family house; 13 were occupied by bachelors, either living on their own or with other unmarried siblings; and 3 were occupied by elder bachelors still living with their parents. The remaining four families are those that can be considered 'pure' cases of nuclear families: two of them were inhabited by men who bought the farm when they married; another inherited the farm from a bachelor uncle before marrying; and the other kept only a few stock on his brother's land. From this emerges a clear pattern of stem family organisation.

However, from what I could observe, I would dare to predict that, given the growing abhorrence to the idea of two families living in the same house, and so long as land continues to be acquired through the same inheritance system, the prevailing pattern for the near future will be that of a nuclear family living in a newly built bungalow beside the old house inhabited by the parents. That is to say, the stem family pattern will continue only if the family is considered as a unit of production, but not as a unit of consumption, since the two generations will remain on the same farm but not in the same house.

The stem family in Ireland has been the object of an interesting debate that I can introduce only very briefly here. In the early ethnography carried out by Arensberg and Kimball in Co. Clare (1937, [1940] 1968), a static stem family system perfectly adapted to the requirements of the farm economy appeared to be the unquestionable model to understand social life in rural Ireland. By now it seems that the historical contingency of the Irish stem family has been widely corroborated (Connell 1968; Symes 1972; O'Neill 1984), not only by historians but also by some anthropologists, who have seen in the marginal family types still prevailing in the far west of the Gaeltacht, 'remnants' of pre-Famine domestic structures very different from that of the stem family (Fox 1978; Taylor 1980).

The controversy about the reality and rationality of the Irish stem family was sparked by Brody's critique (1973) of Arensberg and Kimball's functionalist ideology. Much of that controversy turned on Gibbon and Curtin's thesis, according to which the stem family appeared to be the result of the post-Famine adjustments among the medium farmers. In particular, they argued, it provided a mechanism for the optimisation of labour resources in the context of rural depopulation, which characterised Ireland since the second half of the nineteenth century. This labour optimisation was achieved basically through the unigeniture system of inheritance, which gave rise to the enforced proletarianisation of noninheriting children, becoming thus a cheap source of labour force for the heir; and also, to a lesser extent, through the heir's patrilocal marriage, which involved the addition of the daughter-in-law to the family pool of labour resources (Gibbon 1973; Gibbon and Curtin 1978, 1983).

The empirical accuracy of Gibbon and Curtin's thesis has been questioned by Fitzpatrick (1983), and the theoretical appropriateness of their model has been discussed by Varley (1983) and more recently by Harris (1988). Still, to account for particular inheritance practices (and their associated family models) in terms of their relation with the rationalisation of the labour resources of the domestic unit has proved a useful hypothesis (Habakkuk 1955). The difficulties, perhaps, arise when it comes to explaining what is meant by *rationalisation* of the domestic unit labour resources.

The labour resources of a family farm as they relate to inheritance strategies have to be evaluated, in the first place, according to the availability of land. A reduction of population such as that which ensued after the Famine might increase the ratio of land/inhabitants in a particular area, so that impartible inheritance becomes a more rational strategy for the allocation of noninheriting sons in the uninhabited zones. In the second place, the estimation of the relative availability of land has to be understood in terms of the prevailing type of crop. A shift away from crops with a high level of land productivity, such as potatoes, might strongly dissuade land partibility, since bigger plots are needed for the subsistence of a family (Berkner and Mendels 1978). Again, this trend is precisely what happened in Ireland after the Famine, with the shift from tillage to pastoral farming (cf. Breen 1984). Bearing this in mind, let us have a look at the specific issues involved in the allocation of labour resources within the family unit.

The division of labour that appears to be a result of the family structures is based upon sexual and age differences: a homology between biological features and social categories that easily transmutes cultural arbitrariness into natural determination. Now, the fact that in this context labour is not a commodity should warn us against any abstract model of minimisation of labour expenses or maximisation of its returns, as would be suitable for a market situation. The circulation of labour within a family farm cannot be segregated from the eventualities of the domestic cycle and, more importantly, from the structure of power relations prevailing in the domestic unit. It has been precisely this stress on power relations within the family group at the expense of a narrow economistic determinism that has more consistently challenged, in my view, the early functionalist approaches to the logic of the stem family (see especially Harris 1988).[2] We will have a look at the intrafamily divisions of labour, concentrating first on the most elementary of all divisions of labour, the division of labour by gender.

As has happened in many other modern farming communities, the mechanisation of the farm labour processes has been gradually reducing the involvement of women in farming (see Bouquet 1982; Duggan 1987). Moreover, the practical disappearance of the yard economy has likewise liberated women from one of their traditional drudgeries but, to some extent also, from one of their traditional sources of a certain financial autonomy. 'Aye, women used to work at the land the same as men,' an old farm woman told me, 'tying oats and things like that … And then they had hens and ducks, you see, and they would go to Galway to sell them every week, and they would exchange the eggs for groceries. All that money was to run the house; it would not go to the farm, oh no, the money the man got from the cattle, that would be for him.'[3] 'Women worked much harder in those days,' Paddy O'Brien admits, 'harder than

---

2. 'One can imagine the balance of power shifting in favour of household heads (as against their dependents) sufficiently to transform a stem into an extended family system. Or the reverse might occur, the balance shifting towards children such that a stem family might change into a conjugal family system' (Donham 1981: 537; cf. Laslett 1984).

3. 'As regards income, all money derived from the sale of eggs and butter, the chief concern of the women beyond the house itself, belongs to her to dispose of as she sees fit. Yet the fruits of her labors are also subject to the needs of the family unit, husband and children' (Arensberg and Kimball [1940] 1968: 48).

men, I tell you. Men were at the fields but when they finished they went
to the pub and that was it, but women had to prepare the meals and do
the housework.' Maureen Kennedy, in contrast, thinks that women's
work was not harder than men's but certainly much longer: 'The woman's
hands are never idle' (Arensberg and Kimball [1940] 1968: 38; see also
Harris 1972: 110ff). Whereas now, they do nothing on the farm, Robert
Fox observes; he remembers his mother always doing bits and pieces,
'but now there is machinery, you see, and women have jobs and all that;
hey have no time for the farm.'

People's perceptions of women's work appear, to a great extent, con-
ditioned by the recent past in which it was undoubtedly harder than it
is now. Furthermore, a narrow definition of farm work, prevailing at the
local level but also in the literature on Irish rural society (Shortall 1991),
excludes from its semantic field tasks that are absolutely indispensable
for the implementation of many farm labour processes, such as the feeding of the workers. As far as I could see, it did not seem to me that
women's involvement in farming has disappeared altogether. The problem, however, is that apart from the fact that women never carry out the
main farm jobs (ploughing, cutting hay, silage, etc.), it is hard to discern
any clear pattern as to the degree of women's participation in general
farm work. It is obvious, for instance, that women with small children to
look after will not have much time to help their husbands on the farm.
But this does not mean that once the children have grown up, women
are more likely to participate in farm work. Instead, some will argue that
since the children are already well able to work on the farm, it is they
who have to help the father.

Still, other women do as much as their husbands. Mary Joyce's husband admitted to me that there is no way a farm can thrive if the farmer
does not keep on good terms with his wife. Bridget Burke, on the other
hand, has quite a clear understanding of the reasons for her involvement
in farm work: since her husband gives her a hand with the washing and
all that, she told me, she helps him with the milking of the cows. The
majority argue, however, that they help on the farm just because they
fancy it; for example, Maureen Coppinger, a full-time nurse with three
small children, still finds time to give her husband a hand now and again.
She simply says that she loves to be out. Even those few with no farming
background are just as likely to become involved in their husbands' business, such as Teresa Jordan, the daughter of a forestry worker, who had
never been on a farm until she got married. She proudly asserted that she
never found it too hard to adapt to the farm life, despite the large amount

of work she does there every day. Sometimes it seems, on the contrary, that previous farm experience acts rather as a deterrent to any deep post-marital commitment to farm work, as was the case of Dolores Flaherty.

Dolores was born in a small farm not far from the Three Districts, but very soon she was sent to Dublin to be trained as a nurse. Shortly after her marriage, she inherited thirty-eight acres of land from a childless aunt. At that time, her husband (from a farming background as well) was working in the building trade. Since his job was badly paid, he thought that the farm offered to his wife would help improve his needy economic situation. But Dolores had strong reservations: 'I didn't want to come back because I was reared in a farm; I knew all the work I had to do when I was a kid, no way I would go back to that.' Eventually, she gave in to her husband's pressure, 'and I always regretted it bitterly', even though she put forward three unnegotiable conditions: she would do no work at the farm, she would keep her job, and under no circumstances would a single penny from her salary be invested in the farm. And so it has been ever since, she told me with a certain arrogance.

I think that Dolores's case highlights a very important element in the constitution of the sexual division of labour in family farms. It has to be noted, however, that her solid bargaining situation cannot be generalised. Quite the reverse, the majority of women have to leave their jobs when they get married, and sometimes precisely because of the demands of the farm. This is what happened to Máire Laffey, who left her factory job after getting married because her husband 'wanted somebody at the farm'; and to Maura Finnerty, a nurse too, who stopped working a few years after her marriage. Children had started to arrive by then, she explained, and also her parents-in-law were getting old; they could not help on the farm as much as they had done before, so her husband asked her to leave her job.

Certainly, Dolores's circumstances are not representative, but what we can learn from her experience is that women's involvement in farm work does not depend so much on the life cycle of the family, or the general availability of labour, even though these have their obvious importance too. First and foremost, it depends on that unspoken realm of social relations that constitutes the intimate power structure of the farming family (cf. Whatmore 1991).

This question brings us back to the above-mentioned intersection of the two universes that meet at the family farm. As was pointed out at the beginning of the chapter, the regions of a family farm can be sorted out into two opposing compartments: the farm, belonging to the male sphere, and the house, belonging to the female sphere. This quite rigid sexualisation (or genderisation) of the farm-house complex gives the appearance of the functional interdependence that Arensberg and Kimball were so keen on emphasising:

> Though he [the husband] can make what disposal he will of the funds earned by the labor group, his wife and children can expect as of right that he shall make it for the family as a whole in which each member receives his share. For the work of his wife is complementary to his, and in its own sphere of as great importance to the livelihood and the organisation of the family unit. While he may demand and expect of his wife that she fulfil her household duties, so may she demand and expect that he fulfil his in the management and working of the farm in providing for herself and the children ([1940] 1968: 48).

Both the house and the farm constitute symmetrical and inverse structures of authority. In the same way as the wife is merely an assistant to her husband when she is with him on the farm and she has to work under his orders, the man who ventures into the female domain will have to do so under the rigid supervision of his wife, otherwise he runs the risk of being severely scorned and ridiculed. My friend Pat used to do small jobs in the house garden now and again but, since this belongs to the female sphere, he went there only following his wife's orders. One morning he got so fed up with the work in the garden that he commented to me, half humorously and half bitterly: 'Don't marry a woman who likes gardening!'

Similarly, the care of the children and housework in general is another female domain, the female domain *par excellence*. When my hostess used to come back from Mass on Saturday evening, having left the children with her husband, she would interrogate him about their behaviour and she would tell him off if something did not go as she expected. Had he dared to do any housework in her absence, it would be the object of merciless criticism for the smallest flaw: 'Only a woman can do that!' On the other hand, a woman who fails in her domestic responsibilities, for instance in the discipline of children, will also be censured by her husband; this is parallel to the relentless criticism that a man will receive if he does not comply with his duties. 'I can't stick a man sitting back when there are things to do outside', my hostess used to say whenever she thought that our neighbour's farm was being neglected.

It should be emphasised that the existence of these two spheres does not mean that they do not relate to each other. On the contrary, it has

to be understood as a condition of possibility of their constant interpenetration or, as Strathern would put it (1985), of their mutually constitutive character. A man minding children or doing housework on a regular
basis, that is to say, a man systematically crossing the boundaries of his
male domain, will usually appear in the context of a parallel transcendence of the female sphere by his partner (remember the case of Bridget
Burke mentioned above). There is, therefore, an exchange relationship
between husband and wife; and, like the other exchange relationships we
have been looking at thus far, it is the relative value (exchange value) of
the services in circulation that determines the bargaining position of each
party. In this sense, a woman doing farm work might have a certain
expectation that her husband will give her a hand in her domestic chores.
But the exchange value of her service is certainly much smaller than that
of a woman with an off-farm job, for instance, and consequently, her
expectations of a substantive counter-service are less justified.

It is undoubtedly among families with working wives that I have
observed the deepest penetration of husbands into the female domain.[4]
That is the case of Maureen Coppinger, the full-time nurse whose husband tries to thrive on a thirty-eight-acre farm: 'He does everything in
the house, cooking, washing, cleaning. Only when I am around he can
go to the farm … He never did it before marriage, but now he is well
adapted.' 'But most men around here are not very much into that,'
Dolores Flaherty complains. 'Out in the pub you find them, and the
money earned by their wives all gone in baby-sitters!'[5]

There are only ten women with off-farm jobs in my sample of sixty-
five families (cf. Wickham 1986). Different reasons seem to account for
that fact. On the one hand, patrilocal or 'viri-vicinal' marriage, combined with local exogamy, means that an in-marrying woman will usually find herself living several miles away from her home place and, quite
often, from her original work place too, so this might become much less
accessible. On the other hand, I have already mentioned some cases of
women who left their jobs because their husbands needed their help on

4. See Harris (1984) for an interesting example of the liberating effects of factory
work upon women in a rural community of Co. Mayo.
5. In their highly formalised study of Irish farm families, Hannan and Katsiaouni
do not seem to have found any straightforward relation of reciprocal exchanges
between husband and wife as far as farm and household are concerned. The family
cycle on the one hand, and what they call 'social-emotional integration and leader-
ship' on the other, appear in their view to be the key factors to account for any break
of that traditional division of labour (1977: 122–40).

the farm. Furthermore, as Dolores Flaherty pointed out, not all men are willing to transcend their male domain and help their wives with their domestic duties just for the sake of a few pounds. And last but not least, there is the deep-seated belief, held by both men and women, that the right place for a woman is in her house,[6] that children are spoiled if reared by anyone other than the mother, and that a family loses prestige if the woman needs a job to keep going.

It emerges from this that the interpenetration between the male and female spheres is not a simple matter of a *quid pro quo* exchange. There is, certainly, a functional interdependence between the sexualised productive and reproductive domains of a family farm, but a functional interdependence upheld by a staunch patriarchal structure that women do not seem to find an easy way out of. As I have argued at some length elsewhere (1991), whether they do farm work or not, the life of countrywomen in the Three Districts does not seem particularly attractive. Their gradual marginalisation from the productive sphere, though not absolute, has in any case increased their dependence on their male partners through their confinement within a sterile domestic domain. 'Things have improved alright,' Maureen Coppinger commented to me. 'Women are now able to speak up and all that. But there is still a long way to go; there is no recognition for women who stay in the house, they have no social outlets at all; in fact, nothing has changed for them.'

This opinion seems to contradict recent feminist literature on the situation of women in peasant societies (e.g. Dubisch 1986), especially Susan Rogers's theory of the 'myth of male dominance' (1975). Let me finish very briefly with a quick review of Rogers's assumptions, since this might contribute to a better interpretation of my data on Irish countrywomen.

Susan Rogers developed her theory of the 'myth of male dominance' for European peasant societies on the basis of her fieldwork in northeastern France (1975), following Friedl's original observations in a Greek village as regards the importance of the domestic domain ([1967] 1986: 51). The core of her argument was simple and compelling: since peasant societies seem to be more domestic-oriented than their industrial or urban counterparts, and peasant women play the dominant role in the domestic domain, the alleged patriarchal character of the peasant world can only be a myth; functional to men because it legitimates the rather residual

---

6. And sanctioned by Article 41.2.2 of the Irish Constitution, according to which 'the state shall … endeavour to ensure that mothers shall not be obliged by economic necessity to engage in labour to the neglect of their duties in the home.'

power they enjoy in the public sphere, and functional to women as well because it masks their real power in the domestic sphere (see also Gilmore 1990). Rogers's observations, however, were predicated upon certain structural characteristics – nucleated settlement, partible inheritance, etc. – that by no means can be generalised to the whole of rural Europe, not even rural France, as she herself realised after doing a second fieldwork further south (1985 and 1991). And it is precisely in these structural characteristics that the peasant community she studied substantially differs from the farming community of the Three Districts.

My argument for the subordination of women in Irish rural society is based first of all on the 'depeasantisation' of modern Irish farming communities, especially with reference to the disappearance of the yard economy, which provided women with such an important economic resource. Second of all, apart from losing their peasant character, those farming communities have been traditionally distinguished by three important elements that clearly militate against women's power and autonomy by combining economic expropriation with social isolation: male impartible inheritance, patrilocal residence together with local exogamy and scattered settlement. By and large, it did not seem to me that the farming community of the Three Districts was as domestic-centred as the peasant village studied by Rogers.

Furthermore, while we could argue that the opposition between public and domestic is not identical to that between male and female, the local belief that there is such a parallel has a rather negative effect on women's condition (misrecognition of women's farm work). Such a local belief masks the appropriation of women's labour by their male partners. Again, only a detailed analysis of the nature of the public and domestic domains in a situation of rapid social change, such as that of the west of Ireland, would enable us to arrive at a more definitive conclusion.[7]

7. I cannot fail to mention here the recent publication of the Irish novelist John McGahern (1990), which presents a very vivid picture of patriarchy in Irish rural society. More 'objective' evidence of the gloomy life of Irish countrywomen is provided by Kennedy (1973), who has documented a traditional higher mortality of Irish women as compared with English and American women (pp. 55–56), and a strong female bias in rural emigration (pp. 66–85).

11. Maximising Kinship Relations

*I*f we define patriarchy as a form of social organisation marked by the supremacy of the father in the clan or family, it is clear that women are not the only victims of such a system. Let us have a look at the basic duty of a woman staying in the house, apart from the ever-present housework. Irrespective of the role that they can play in the process of production as such, the appropriate task for Irish countrywomen in the reproductive sphere seems less controversial. 'This evening they began disputing about their wives,' Synge observed of his Aran islanders, 'and it appeared that the greatest merit they see in a woman is that she should be fruitful and bring them many children' ([1907] 1979: 122). 'No matter how much money you have,' a woman from Inagh said to Arensberg, 'no matter how good looking you are, if you don't have children, you are no good. But if you are ugly as the worst and have children, you are all right' (1937: 90). He even documented the existence of a 'country divorce', in virtue of which a man could send a barren wife back to her parents and give the land to one of his brothers in return for a sum of money on condition that the brother had to marry and have descendants (p. 91). But why has it been so important for country men to maximise the fertility of their wives?

We will focus our attention now on the other fundamental criterion for the categorisation of family members, and thus, for the constitution of intrafamily relations of production, namely, generation. The well-documented high marital fertility of the Irish[1] does not seem to have a

---

1. Taking into account the farm manager's family of origin, my sample gives an average family size of 5.7 (cf. Breen, Hannan, Rottman and Whelan 1990: 113–16.

commonly agreed on explanation. To see it as the consequence of the use of children as labour force in family farms (e.g. Harris 1972: 64–65) has not fully convinced everyone (Kennedy 1973: 201). Curtin and Varley have found three main reasons for the desire for children in rural Ireland, according to the ethnographic literature: generational continuity ('keeping the name on the land'), labour for family farms, and a hedge against old age (1984: 31–32).[2] Whatever their relative importance might be, it is interesting to note that, parallel to the decreasing significance of children's labour in family farms, there has also been a reduction of the average family size (Breen, Hannan, Rottman and Whelan 1990: 113–16). Similarly to what we saw for women, the mechanisation of the farm labour processes explains why children are now less needed as a labour force supply. And similarly as well to what we find in the ethnographic literature, my Irish friends are far from unanimous when it comes to accounting for the phenomenon of big families.

'Well, they didn't have any other amusement than sex at that time,' Noel Forde told me, himself coming from a family with nine children. 'They were very poor, you see, and in all poor countries people have lots of children … Lack of education, that's what it is.' 'It was crazy really,' Kate Sheridan affirmed, who has five children herself, 'but that was their belief, they didn't have anything else to do!' People were self-sufficient, Joe Connor observed, and 'it was not that expensive to rear a family in those days.' Denis Jordan agreed with Joe: 'There were few expenses at that time, people ate what they produced, they would only eat meat ten times a year perhaps, when they killed some beast. Now a man with eleven or twelve children either he is very rich or he will be very poor.' Paddy Kelly believed that families were big because more hands made the work lighter; he also suggested that the living conditions were so poor that people had plenty of children lest they lose a few: 'Look at Africa now, families are big there too, it's poverty that makes people have big families.' For Máire Laffey, on the other hand, it was because there were no contraceptive methods available. She told me that her mother, who had twelve children, asked the doctor many times for contraceptives; but he was an old man, the old-fashioned type, so he did not want to give them to her. He said that she was a healthy woman, so she could keep having children, without any bother. 'And there is the religion too,' she adds. 'They say that you cannot receive the Holy Communion if you

2. Cf. the reasons for low fertility in historical England according to Macfarlane (1986: 51ff).

practice contraception.' Robert Grealish also remarked on religion; he remembers that not long ago the priest would ask you in confession when you had had the last baby, and how it was that you did not have any more; 'but this thing is dying out', he concluded.

Whether this is a plausible explanation or not, and maybe at the risk of venturing into a too functionalist argument, my evidence suggests that a lavish progeny is particularly useful on a family farm. In the olden days (before the generalised mechanisation of the productive processes), it was a very common practice to exchange children as labour force among neighbours. This is what Arensberg noted as 'lending a boy' (1937: 64–65; see also Williams 1956: 40). Old Ger Badger explained it to me: 'Going back years, neighbours used to send their sons to work for other neighbours, you know, for one or two days; the lads would be working and they would be fed there, and go home at night.' Mary Burke claimed that her brothers did a lot of work for other farmers: 'Daddy used to say: "Go and help this or that", they might get a few pounds, but usually nothing.' 'Aye, we were sent out by father,' Paddy Joe Coppinger remembered, 'and you had to go, whether you liked it or not … You wouldn't get paid, your father would then get help from other lads, you see.' Bridget Morris had very bad memories of her father's work strategies: 'We were kept at the farm, but I didn't want to do to my children what was done to me, that is why I have educated them. But my father kept us all at home. He died a few years ago being a wealthy man, all thanks to our work. And we got nothing!'

The usefulness of a big family in traditional rural society, not only as a source of labour but also as a source of currency to obtain labour, is quite apparent. We can also understand from this why intergenerational antagonisms, which Arensberg and Kimball did not fail to notice ([1940] 1968: 55–58), have been so salient in Irish literature (e.g. Synge [1907] 1983). All signs of that exploitation of children have certainly disappeared at present. Still, their contribution to the labour resources of a farm should not be neglected, and neither can intergenerational frictions be relegated to a mere thing of the past. I have found on many occasions bitter feelings between father and son working on the same farm, especially when the father has not yet surrendered full control over the business, and the son is coming to an age when he likes to make his own decisions. But as Brody has pointed out (1973: 109–30), the demise of the farm economy has been gradually undermining the material basis of much of the father's authority over his family. Let me now convey a little of the work atmosphere in a farming family that I know well.

June and July are busy months in Jim Egan's house. The saving of the turf, together with the hay, keeps his people occupied most of the time during the summer months. Jim is in his late sixties; he lives with his wife and three unmarried adult children, Seán, Paula and Una, but he has four more daughters and two more sons, all married and living away. Two of them, however, Jimmy and Mary, are not too far from the home place; both were given sites from the old man's land on getting married. Jimmy also keeps a few cattle on his father's land and grows a few potatoes. When it is time to save the turf, the three neighbouring families pool their work so that they can all have a little of the traditional fuel for their respective hearths, and in fact all the members of the family except Paddy, who lives in Co. Kildare, come along at some stage to help out in exchange for a bit of turf. The same happens at hay time, even though there is no clear payment for the family help at this time, since Jim keeps all the harvest for himself. In any case, we can very well end up having as many as twenty people working in Jim Egan's fields, both adults and kids, children and grandchildren.

Not everybody enjoys the gratifications of collective work in the same way, though. Both Bridie, a daughter married to a part-time farmer, and Eileen, another one recently married to a cattle dealer, complained bitterly about the hard work they have to do every summer: 'This is not holidays … and for all we get we might as well stay at home!' But Teresa, married to a factory worker, does not agree with her sisters: 'We have a good crack there, all the family working together. You don't feel the time passing, really.' Whether they like it or not, most of them go every year, even if it is just 'to give a hand to the old lad'.

We find all sorts of different combinations of family labour, both nuclear and extended, in the turf and hay saving. Teresa and her husband, to give just another example, decided to rent a plot of bog some years ago. Since at that time they did not have any family labour for the work, two of Teresa's brothers, Jimmy and Seán, came to help out. However, they did not receive any turf in exchange, just the meals for the day. This was probably on the understanding that family reciprocities do not have to be paid off straight away, since they flow in a taken-for-granted circuit of indefinitely delayed returns.

Yet as soon as the work of the nuclear family is available, this generally (but not necessarily) takes precedence over that of the extended family. Particularly for the turf, children, no matter how young these might be, constitute the basic source of work in the nuclear family. If we think about the nature of the work involved in turf saving, we will easily understand why children are so suitable for its implementation. In fact, anyone in the family who is not disabled gives a hand, but children seem to fit in particularly well. Turf saving does not require any physical strength, special concentration, or specific skills, and school very rarely constitutes a socially acceptable excuse to escape from the work at the bog.[3] Joe Maloney, for instance, is another small farmer with four young children, two boys of twelve and seven and two girls of eight and four. Except for the small girl, they are all at school, but they are all eager to forget about their lessons when the time comes to go to the bog, except for the eldest girl, Brigid, who never fancied the saving of the turf. 'She is spoilt,' neighbours commented disapprovingly, 'how come that all the rest are at the bog while herself goes to school? Too much pressure on education now, that's what happens ... ' There is no golden rule, it seems to me, as to whether children are obliged to help at the bog. It all depends on how much the parents are interested in getting the job finished as soon as possible, how many alternative sources of work they might have, or how they evaluate the missed school days in comparison with the turf.

We can visualise from these examples a genuine picture of what a family business consists. It is important to underline here how the nuclear family can be widely extended, including sons, daughters, brothers and sisters of the farm manager who once were living in the same house, and their respective children. Many of these are not farming families, but this does not seem to make any difference when it is a matter of giving a hand to the brother or to the father on the old family farm, provided that they do not happen to live too far away, or in any case, that they are willing to spend a few days of their holidays in the healthy countryside.

In fact, the availability of family labour determines quite directly the viability of many farm enterprises. Jim McCann used to grow a large potato crop when his children were around, but now that they are all gone he does not regard it as profitable any more. Similarly, Pat Sheridan has to buy all his turf cut and saved; he has five children living in his house plus his wife and an unmarried sister, but the simple fact is that they are not willing to help. Sometimes the lack of family assistance can be compensated for by other forms of work, but this is not always practical. On the other hand, if it is undeniable that the availability of family labour shapes

---

3. See John McGahern (1963: 126) for a very moving account of children's work at the bog.

the farm enterprise, it is no less true that the farm enterprise bears conspicuously upon the constitution of the farming family itself. Families can be extended not only 'naturally' to suit the demands of farming but also 'fictively' through the well-known practices of fosterage and adoption (cf. Goody 1976: 66ff; 1983: 68ff, 191). Unfortunately, I cannot bring quantitative information as to the extension of those practices in the west of Ireland. But from my informants' accounts, I would guess that they are quite widespread and, furthermore, that they are directly related to the slippery question of illegitimacy. Insufficient data, however, prevent me from developing this any further (see Salazar 1994).

In any case, the mutually constitutive character of family and farm stands out once again with crystal clarity. As Arensberg and Kimball observed, 'for the farm family, farm work is as much a family matter as is sharing the same table' ([1940] 1968: 50).[4] The two spheres that intersect at the family farm, which I defined as male and female in the context of the sexual division of labour, appear now under a different heading. In this context, the nuclear family, the extended family and the kinship network are all evocative of the initial female domain, and they all incorporate their specific social obligations within which the economic demands of the farm, metamorphosis of the male sphere, have to be met. The same contradiction between the two spheres emerges again but with a distinctive dimension, thus adding a new connotation to the original meaning. The kinship system provides a dense web of routes and passages along which the services and counter-services of the farm economy can circulate side by side with and be exchanged for, or be exchanged into, a different order. 'As in other cases of petty commodity production,' Long noticed among Peruvian farmers, 'kinship and quasi-kinship ties often provide the basic normative context for the organisation of labour; this tends to infuse work relations with value contents deriving from wider fields of social relations' (1986: 90).

It is necessary to explore the specificity of the kinship universe if we are to understand the value contents that kinship infuses into the organisation of labour. Kinship comprises an order of social relations that not only

4. 'The bourgeois urban dwellers, who limit the elementary social unit to the nuclear family, perceive the existence of a wide rift between the realm of the economic and the realm of the familial. For the peasant such a split makes no sense: the casa is not only a unit of production and consumption, it is also a unit of production and property. The spheres of the economic and the familial, which for the bourgeoisie are antonymical and almost irreconcilable, are inseparable for the rural minhoto.' (Pina-Cabral 1986: 38).

endows the farm economy with a social framework, but also contains its own system of exchanges. The type of reciprocities that circulate within the kinship network has a strong flavour of domesticity, of the female domain, of the emotional, without, however, being completely reducible to it. Let us have a quick look at them. We have, first of all, the rites of passage: christenings, holy communions, confirmations and weddings. They all give rise to profuse gift exchanges among both kin and neighbours. A newly wed couple does not have to buy most of the house gadgets, since these are given as presents by their relations (on condition that they are invited to the wedding). The same applies to a mother with a new-born baby as regards the child's clothes, apart from the fact that children's clothes are usually swapped among relatives and neighbours once they have been outgrown. In addition, and particularly related to the female sphere, the kinship network also provides a channel for the circulation of specific obligations concerning the care of elderly parents and, similarly, for the exchange of baby-sitting services.

The existence of an elderly parent or couple prevents many unmarried women from pursuing their professional careers for the sake of their family obligations. This was the case of Kate Sheridan, who had to return from England and give up her nursing studies because she had to take care of her widowed mother. And after marriage, it is very often the care of their husband's parents that does not allow women to keep their jobs; even though their sacrifice might have been somehow compensated by the baby-sitting services that the old couple provided when they were still able. Parallel to this female responsibility, on the other hand, could be considered the situation of many young men who had to pack in their jobs after being called by their fathers to look after the family farm. Damian Forde was doing quite well in England working at the buildings until his father told him that he needed him at the farm. He went back to Ireland straightaway. 'I was the only one who came when the old two wanted someone to look after them and the farm', he said to me, trying to explain why he got the family land instead of any other of his brothers. And the same inescapable duties seem to have fallen upon Jimmy Doherty, a middle-aged bachelor living with his parents; when I asked him if he ever thought of giving up farming, he simply stated that 'somebody has to mind the old folks', clearly implying that he saw his farming condition as a result of his family obligations.

It goes without saying that this system of exchanges internal to the family unit does not preclude the development of sharp intergenerational conflicts and antagonisms, parallel to those I have already mentioned in the context of the organisation of farm work. As a matter of fact, many such frictions clearly derive from the very development of the taken-for-granted system of family reciprocities. We might better understand then why the majority of young people refuse so convincingly the idea of living with their parents after marriage. It is as if they were attempting to separate the economic sphere, the farm, wherein the coexistence of two generations is practically unavoidable, from the emotional sphere, the family, wherein such coexistence might be perceived as less imperative. This attempt is never fully successful given the conditions of a community of family farms.

Kinship obligations, on the other hand, do not fall only upon those living in the same house. The family unit has a paramount responsibility as regards the care of the elders; there are other forms of assistance, however, that circulate within the kinship network too but well beyond the boundaries of both nuclear and stem families. This is the case of baby-sitting services, which leads us back once again to the female domain. Relatives, both kin and affines, take care of each other's children quite frequently, and the closer they are the better.

Neighbours can also participate but only when they keep on very good and intimate terms. Whenever she wanted to go out, my hostess Teresa Kelly used to leave her two small children with her sister Bridie, who is married to a small farmer near Galway city, more than fifteen miles away. When I asked her if it would not be better to leave the children with someone living a bit nearer, she said that she would never leave them with anyone outside her family. Then she mentioned her next-door neighbour Máire Maloney, but she has four children herself whereas Bridie has none, so it is better to leave them with Bridie. We should not forget that even though these services do not have to be 'paid off' straightaway, they certainly create an expectation of reciprocity that will have to be met sooner or later. 'We have to keep Bridie happy', my hostess said once her husband had gone to do some small repairs at Bridie's place, 'otherwise she won't baby-sit for us'. The eventuality of having to look after Máire's four children as a counter-service probably dissuaded Teresa from relying too much on her neighbour's assistance.

As we will see in the next chapter, the spheres of kinship and neighbourhood overlap on many occasions, but they are far from coincident. There is something distinctively unique in a blood relationship that no other form of arrangement can substitute for. Take, for instance, the case of fosterage and adoption. No matter how popular these practices are in this region, the sort of fictive kinship that they create is never confused with the real blood relationship. This was so emphatically asserted to me that I cannot fail to note it here. But what does a blood relationship have, we might ask, that makes it so different from any other type of tie? For the time being, the only way we can answer that question is by reference to the specific set of moral values normally associated with a kinship link. It is from its capacity to agglutinate in a single bond a myriad of different 'spheres of exchange' that a kinship relationship obtains its moral strength. These are the different spheres of exchange that I have been trying to show in the previous paragraphs.[5]

Let us consider now the significance of kinship after all we have seen thus far. 'They think the claim of kinship more sacred than the claims of abstract truth', Synge observed in the Aran islands ([1907] 1979: 64). 'It is a family that you marry, not just a woman', Pádraig claimed. 'I never had problems with my contractor', said Paddy Morris, 'because the man is related to me, you see.' The significance of kinship in rural communities has puzzled anthropologists ever since the very moment that they started to look away from their beloved 'primitives'. Once it became clear that kinship relations did not play the overwhelming role that they were so fond of underscoring among the so-called simple societies, but at the same time it became clear that it could not be understood as a mere version of kinship in urban capitalist formations, a liminal space between 'simple' and 'complex' structures started to take shape for which classical anthropological theory did not seem to provide adequate analytical tools (cf. Segalen 1986: 61–72).

Concerning the type of exchanges specifically defined as belonging to the kinship sphere, the role of kinship relations in rural communities does not seem to differ substantially from what can be observed in modern urban contexts (cf. Young and Willmott [1957] 1986). But these are not the only services that circulate throughout the kinship network. According to Medick and Sabean, the kin network appears as a mechanism through which all sorts of different resources can be mobilised (1984: 21). Cohen maintains that 'it is a means of justifying one's choice of close social associates from a potentially unlimited universe of associates' (1987: 68). 'A panel of candidates' is what the family offers to the

---

5. 'What kinship does, as reflected in patterns of behaviour, the formation of groups (through criteria of recruitment emphasising one line of descent) and their activities, does not explain why it should do it unless we accept some kind of moral force behind it. This force, moral or otherwise, cannot be explained as a function of what kinship does without tautology' (Bouquet and De Haan 1987: 254). It does not seem to me that there is any answer to such a question formulated in those terms.

Mexican peasant, according to Foster. 'He selects (and is selected by) relatively few with whom the significant working relationships are developed' (1961: 1181). And in a similar fashion, Pitt-Rivers defines kinship in southern Spain as a 'facultative rather than a firm bond' (1971: 106), and he claims that only when it is associated 'with political structure, locality or economic production, one is accustomed to find that the extensions of the elementary family are endowed with structural importance' (p. 103).[6]

They all seem to agree that the weight of the kinship network in rural communities is unquestionable *as long as* it can be related to something else, i.e., as long as it can be coextensive with another type of social structure for which it will provide, in Cohen's words, a rhetoric of legitimation, and from which it will obtain, in Pitt-River's words, structural importance. The analysis of kinship per se, therefore, becomes a pointless exercise unless it is linked with that of those other social relationships.

I would only add, however, that in my view this process is two-fold. In other words, if it is certainly true that kinship acquires its structural importance from extrakinship spheres, these extrakinship spheres acquire in turn a distinctive tone from their association with the kinship system because, let us say it again, kinship incorporates a set of meanings and values (or forms of social exchange) that make it irreducible to any other social universe. Let me leave this as a provisional conclusion; I will return to it in Chapter 13.

6. As for Irish ethnography, parallel arguments have recently been put forward by Harris in her critical review of the stem family debate (1988; see also Hannan 1972, 1979 and Leyton 1975).

12. The Social Life of Space

*T*he other category of social relationships with a role analogous to that of kinship is neighbourhood. As other students of western Ireland have pointed out, despite all the 'modernising' changes that have been affecting the rural communities for so long, the primary ascriptive groups of kinship and neighbourhood still constitute the most significant networks of interaction (Hannan and Katsiaouni 1977: 86–87). Like kinship, neighbourhood also seems to have this power to assimilate in a singular link all sorts of different forms of social exchange. There is also a moral effect of this integrative capacity, but with a less emotional and more diffuse content. It is a moral effect that sometimes stands out precisely when its principles have been broken.

Let us have a look at the following report on a dispute over the ownership and use of bog land that was once brought before Tuam Court. An old-age pensioner was charged with damaging his neighbour's fencing so as to gain access to a bog that he claimed was rightfully his. The plaintiff stated that he owned a large area of bog at Cloonascragh on which he cut turf and grazed horses. He said that he saw the defendant demolishing the fencing that enclosed the animals and throwing it down a drain. 'He approached people that I have sold plots of turf to', went on the denouncer, 'and said that they should be paying him for them and not me. He goes around letting plots of my land and pretending he owns it.' Against this accusation the defendant claimed that he had been there for the last sixty years, whereas the other had arrived only a few years before. 'I removed the wire and pallets', he argued, 'to make my way into my bog. Dowd [the plaintiff] came along in his van and told me to go away. He threw me to the ground and I hurt my elbow … We are in that bog for generations. We always cut turf there. I even cut a trailer with the *sleán* last year. I am doing nothing wrong in going into my own turf.' The judge, Justice John Garavan, remarked that it was hard to believe that there was not enough room for the neighbours to live in harmony with all the people who were emigrating (*Tuam Herald*, 25 May 1991).

Neighbourhood provides a stage for social interaction, for social cooperation and, by extension, for social conflict. In this chapter I am concerned with the analysis of the different ways in which neighbourhood as a physical space is rendered socially meaningful. Social conflict is one of these ways; as a matter of fact, social conflict can be seen as another form of reciprocal relationship in which the items exchanged are to the detriment and not to the advantage of the parties involved. Interesting parallels can be drawn between intracommunity contentions, negative exchanges, we might call them, and the rest of reciprocal relations, the positive exchanges.[1]

In the Three Districts, as in all human communities, frictions, quarrels, altercations, fights, and even feuds constitute an integral part of the local social scene. I know two families there who have not talked to each other for two generations; the bog again seems to be at the origins of this old feud. People say that long ago there was a row about trespassing rights, which has been handed down to the present owners. The overlapping of different types of *ius in rem* on the same object (Chapter 2) explains to some extent why the use of bog land has given rise to so many conflicts. But it is not only the bog and its jural complexities that embitter neighbourhood relationships.

Disputes over land ownership are very likely to crop up whenever antagonistic interests happen to develop. That was the case between John Costello and the publican Patrick Fitzgerald. There was a vacant site right behind Patrick's pub where John used to graze his cattle. When Patrick was making some refurbishments in his pub, the workers began to throw debris on the nearby site, much to John's anger, who then claimed that the land was his and that they did not have any right to throw anything on it. The case was brought to court, and eventually John lost his *de facto* grazing rights and he had to pay a huge amount of money, whether as judicial fees or as some sort of restitution, people do

---

1. Cf. Campbell's study of the reciprocal relationships between theft and countertheft among the Sarakatsani (1964: 211–12).

not know; but the bitter feelings between the two families are not a secret to anyone.

'I once saw John Costello fighting against six men', Noel Forde remembered. 'Aye, he was a good fighter ... I can't think of the reason now. I'd say it was because of cattle grazing in somebody else's land or something like that.' In years gone by, if there was an argument between two people, Noel explained, they would not go to court, as they do now, they would just fight. When two men wanted to initiate a fight, let's say at a fair, they would start shouting abuse at each other from a distance, then one of them would walk the 'half way' and would wait for the other one to do likewise, and so the fight would start. 'It was like a ritual ... but they would not last for long; you could fight a man today and be good friends again tomorrow.' Thirty or forty years ago the guards did not pay attention to those fights, they were so frequent; everything could be sorted out with a fight. And they would take place in any type of gathering: fairs, dance-halls, even pilgrimages. There is an ancient holy well on top of a hill, Tobar Phadraig, they call it. It is used as a graveyard now, but in olden times, when it came the patron day, it was a favourite site for pilgrimages and faction fights.[2] 'That was the usual thing,' Noel's wife points out. 'It was a kind of sport at that time; now they have hurling, then fights.'

Still, fights have not disappeared altogether, even though they might have lost much of their sporting spirit. After some months of living in the Three Districts, I came to know that a neighbour of mine, whom I had never been able to see, was serving a sentence in Dublin prison. 'He beat one of the Clarkes so badly that he left him thinking that he was dead,' a man told me, 'but he wasn't dead, so your man was denounced and he ended up in prison.' The Clarkes are a family of landless ex-farm labourers (now factory workers) who live just half a mile down the road from my hosts. One of their girls used to get a lift to work from the brother of the man who is now in prison; after the incident she went on getting her lifts all the same, but her good neighbour had to break almost all relations with his brother's family. There is no way we can separate interfamily conflicts from the general circulation of interfamily reciprocities. And the principles that hold in both cases look strikingly similar.

2. 'On these patron days,' we read in an account of the early nineteenth century, 'which generally fall out on Sundays, great numbers of young persons of both sexes assemble, tents are erected, music, dancing, drinking and every kind of excess takes place, and the revel not infrequently terminates in battery and bloodshed, from the contention of adverse factions' (quoted by Evans 1957: 263).

We will remember that in relations of mutual assistance it was suggested that the identity of the subjects was far more important than the objects exchanged. Does this rule apply to neighbourhood conflicts too? One of the most common incidents likely to spark a quarrel between neighbours is when livestock break into somebody else's land. Interestingly, however, people admit that there is nothing particularly grave in that; it all depends on who is the owner of the land and who is the owner of the cattle. Once Pat's sheep broke into one of his first cousin's fields; the two flocks got mixed up, so they had to be gathered, driven to the farmyard and checked one by one. Both Pat and his kinsman spent several hours at it, but no argument or bad mood arose as a result. On another occasion, there were cattle on the road; 'That must be Hogan's cattle,' Pat commented to me. 'He is as careless, that fellow! And it's dangerous, you know, for the cars … and they also might pull out other people's cattle.' But eventually we found out that it was Tomás Finnerty's cattle that had gone astray and not Hogan's. 'Well, Tomás is a good farmer,' Pat conceded. 'I'm sure it won't happen again.'

A similar episode took place on Noel Forde's farm with his bullocks. They knocked down one of the stone walls and broke into a neighbour's field; it is very easy to get them running, and very often they become very agitated. Some crops the neighbour had growing over there were damaged by Noel's cattle. But he is a 'decent man', Noel remarked, so he did not have to offer any compensation; he only had to rebuild the stone wall and that was it. But what would have happened had the neighbour not been so 'decent'? Noel did not have the same luck when shortly afterward his bull burst its way through an electric fence and inseminated somebody else's heifer. He and his wife went to collect it straightaway and came back with worried expressions. The heifer was not supposed to get in calf, so this time Noel was afraid that he might have to compensate the heifer's owner. But according to other people's comments, that would be unusual; on the contrary, most farmers would have only been too glad to have their heifers bulled without having to pay for it. But Noel's neighbour held an entirely different opinion.

We see again how the language of farm work objectifies interpersonal relationships; whether these are relations of cooperation or relations of conflict does not make much difference. The point I want to make here is that in both cases, neighbourhood operates as a common denominator. Many of the clashes I have been reporting would not have taken place, in the same way at least, had the subjects lived far away from each other. The fact of living in the same neighbourhood, in the same physical space, does not by itself mean that confrontation is more likely to develop, but the existence of those conflicts can certainly be taken as an indication that a particular social formation permeates the edges of an otherwise inert locality.

In a community of small farmers, physical proximity has a deep social meaning; the neighbour is not just the person who lives 'down there', but the person with whom much of day-to-day interaction takes place, either positive or negative, cooperative or competitive. 'In Ashworthy', Williams reminds us, 'a farmer's neighbours are those people who cooperate with him and his immediate family in certain well-defined ways during the every-day running of the farm and household' (1963: 100). The Irish word for neighbour, *comharsa*, is cognate with the word we already know for cooperation, *comhar* (*comhar na gcomharsan*: mutual aid given by neighbours). It would be mistaken, however, to infer from this a simple correlation between physical distance and social space. 'The dispersal of habitations exercises some influence on neighbourliness between farmers,' argues Williams. 'The numerous face-to-face contacts which are typical of village neighbours, for example, are obviously absent'; and yet 'many of the more important aspects of neighbourliness, among them mutual aid in day-to-day activities and behaviour in crisis situations, are more highly developed among farmers than among villagers' (1956: 144). It is the specific social context that renders physical proximity socially meaningful, and not the other way around.

The constitution of neighbourhood as a socially significant physical space, on the other hand, does not result from the operation of a single principle. It stems rather from the interaction of several factors, each of them conferring upon the underlying space a particular meaning. I have said that neighbourhood provides a stage for different forms of social relationships, but these different forms of social relationships might as well define their respective 'neighbourhoods' in different ways, sometimes overlapping, sometimes intersecting.

Relations of neighbourhood, networks of cooperation among farmers and the kinship system all have ego-centred structures. We have already seen some of the consequences that can be derived from this structural homology. Ott observed among Basque shepherds that to the corporate organisation of interhousehold cooperation corresponded a rigid demarcation of neighbourhood boundaries for each household (Ott 1981: 63–81). In the west of Ireland, in contrast, cooperative practices lack any formal regulation, and similarly, the extent of one's neighbourhood is neither explicit nor clear. Apart from this, the ego-centred structure of each household's network clashes with two types of nucleated (super)-structures: the administrative districts and the parish, which, to make things more complex, do not even coincide, as we know from the Introduction. It is the boundaries of the parish that concern our present discussion, because they too confer social significance on the physical space that they define.

The limits of the parish include a socially significant space considerably larger than the ego-centred neighbourhood of each household. And they are very likely to cut across the neighbourhoods of those households situated at the border of that space. 'They don't go to Mass here, you see; I don't know her … ', my landlady told me when I asked her about the wife of a farmer who lived at the other side of the parish border. Furthermore, each parochial space is then broken down into what they call 'station areas', which might include between fifteen and twenty households. Twice a year, from April to June and from October to December, a Mass is celebrated in a different house of each one of those station areas. This is an ancient tradition that dates from Penal Times (eighteenth century) and has been kept alive in rural areas ever since. When the Stations take place in a house, all the neighbours of its corresponding station area are invited, and they all help in the preparations. The priest comes along to say Mass and to listen to confessions, and afterward the woman of the house cooks a big meal for all those present. Once the priest is gone, the party might well last until very late at night.

Depending on how big the parish is, the same house normally has Stations every four or five years. People say that it is a good opportunity to carry out refurbishments. Despite its religious significance, everybody is aware that the Stations constitute a social event, an opportunity to make home improvements and an opportunity for women to meet and exchange gossip, since it is mostly women who participate. The last time Stations took place in my neighbourhood, I heard women complaining that the priest 'stayed for too long', so they could not pursue their more profane interests until late.

As a matter of fact, the majority of religious rituals, and attending Mass stands out prominently among them, go well beyond the mere fulfilment of a religious obligation. Through the weekly duty of Mass attendance the social dimension of the parish becomes apparent, irrespective, to some extent, of its religious content. At the end of each service, the parish priest always makes some announcements in relation to community affairs, not necessarily related to religious matters: the setting up of bingo in the village, a meeting of schoolchildren's parents or the water scheme committee – even the arrival of a foreign anthropologist can enter public knowledge in that way.

These examples show the social/secular imprint of religious institutions in rural Ireland. But it is not the outspoken social functions of the church that I am interested in now. There is no straightforward answer to the simple question of why people go to Mass; it is necessary to participate regularly in the enactment of that social ritual if one wants to find out any evidence of its object. 'That the remarkably large attendances at rural churches and chapels', Evans observes, 'owe something to the social needs of a scattered population is suggested by the phrase, applied to someone who arrives late at chapel: "he missed the Mass but hit the gathering" – he had something worth while for his trouble' (1957: 253).

The people of the Three Districts celebrate a particular 'subversion' of the Holy Mass that they ironically call the 'outdoor Mass'. Every Sunday, while the service is being held inside the church, groups of men gather outside, either at the church door or a few yards further away. They talk and smoke until the Mass is over, and then they move to the local pub. Noel, who is a faithful church-goer, tells me that on the few occasions he has decided to stay outside with the lads instead of going into church, he has known in a few minutes everything that was going on in the community, so effective are the gossip networks. It is important to notice, on the other hand, that, unlike the Stations, this is an exclusively male domain: women never participate in the outdoor Mass.

I asked Noel why it is that men stay outside the church. 'That comes from the Penal Times,' he answered; people were not allowed to attend Catholic Masses in those days, so whenever Mass was celebrated they had to have out-lookers to raise the alarm if they saw the English coming. That is why the men don't go in; it is an old custom that has been handed down from generation to generation. An interesting rationalisation, I thought, although not everybody agrees with it. 'Never heard of that', another man told me when I put Noel's theory to him; 'I'd say it is the neighbours coming in they want to keep an eye on, that's why they stay outside', he added humorously. It might well be that the ancient tradition remembered by Noel has some bearing on these outdoor meetings at Mass time, but what the other man said hints at a deeply felt connotation of church-going, which turns it into a sort of dramatic display of community membership over which a pervasive social control is exercised.

'It's a shame that so many people go to Mass just to show off,' complained one of my neighbours. 'They all go there with their new suits ...

but what will you get from God if you wear a new suit? I wonder, what will you get from the priest?' And then they would talk and talk if they missed you at Mass too often. Definitely, neighbours do not like it if somebody does not go to Mass, 'but they wouldn't be too hostile either', a farm woman remarked. 'Aye, there would be gossip among neighbours if a nondisabled person did not go to Mass', confirmed another one. And then she went on telling me that her husband once spent the whole Saturday plastering the walls of a shed. 'You'd better go to Mass tomorrow and forget about your plastering,' she said to him. 'The neighbours will talk if you are working all day: "this one did not go to Mass and now he is working."' Others, on the other hand, have an entirely cynical view: 'Bah!, it's very easy to cheat them,' a man claimed. 'You only have to go out every Sunday morning and come back within an hour or so, that's all you need.'

Widespread ownership of private cars has increased the possibilities of dodging the neighbours' check over one's church-going habits: people of the same parish do not necessarily have to attend Mass at the same church if they do not wish. This has certainly challenged the effectiveness of the parish as a socially meaningful space. Still, the very fact that you 'have to cheat' your neighbours if you want to keep them quiet strikes me as quite significant. 'It's all hypocrisy!' said a young farmer. 'Most of them wouldn't go if they were in a city where nobody went.' 'Do you mean that people go to Mass just because everybody goes?' I enquired. 'Almost!' he replied. 'People go to Mass to avoid gossip, but this is only for the locals, you see; if one of them commuters doesn't go they would take no notice of it.' This last observation hints at an important point. It is not so much the nucleated space of the parish as such that is more effective in terms of social control, but rather the overlapping of that space with the ego-centred neighbourhoods of each household that confers upon church-going its quasi-compulsory character. That is why the church-going surveillance affects only the 'locals'.

I have been trying to convey to the reader a little of the stifling atmosphere that religious bonds can create in a small community. The point here is that those religious prescriptions – superstructures, if you like – would not be half as effective were it not for their interaction with the secular infrastructures of the community itself, with its internal power relations. Church-going can be seen as a means of social control, not so much of the church over the parishioners, but rather of the parishioners over one another. I do not think I am pushing the argument too far when I say that it is the secular community and not the church that makes it compulsory for people to go to Mass. And in so doing, the physical space demarcated by the concept of neighbourhood appropriates a new function.

Neighbourhood provides an essential stage not only for social cooperation, or social conflict, but also for social control, by means of its overlapping with the wider space provided by the parochial boundaries. In other words, it could be said that religious institutions, practices, beliefs and rituals all become instruments for the implementation of specific internal functions of the neighbourhood, idioms for the verbalisation of its unspoken meanings. But what internal condition, we could wonder, what infrastructural element operates in collusion with those superstructural prescriptions so as to make social control effective? I have already referred to it in passing when I was talking about the Stations and the outdoor Mass.

If there is any sense in which the social meaning of neighbourhood as a physical space becomes more dramatically apparent, this is through its redoubtable gossip networks. Neighbourhood social control could never be implemented were it not for an effective system for the circulation of critical information. No one living in the Three Districts could fail to notice a deep awareness of the gossip threat, an ever-present eagerness to protect one's privacy against neighbours' intrusions. My landlady, an in-marrying woman from another parish further west, seemed to be particularly sensitive in that line. 'Visitors come at any time of the day and there is nothing to put them off,' she used to complain to me at the beginning. 'It's very annoying really, especially when you have a few jobs to do and somebody comes in, you have to chat them up, you cannot just leave them … If you feel tired you cannot just draw the curtains and lock the door, somebody is going to be knocking at sooner or later, and they get angry if you don't let them in!' After a while, I started to realise that such omnipresent visitors were more imaginary than real. And yet, so common and widely felt was the fear of them.

Similarly to what we saw with reciprocal cooperation, this negative aspect of neighbourliness was also defined as 'very Irish,' but with the added connotation of backward, primitive, uncivilised, etc. which are also usually associated with Irishness. 'Here people are very conscious of one another', Noel told me. 'They are afraid of just going for a walk along the road,' he explained, 'because neighbours would say that they have nothing to do, that they have no work; would you believe it?' There is a great fear of neighbours' knowing too much about one's business. Noel said that in the meetings organised by the water scheme, most of the people never speak up; they prefer to arrange things privately with the members of the committee because they do not want other people to know about their dealings. But what is really seen as backward, then? Sometimes one would say that it is not the real existence of gossip but its imaginary threat, or maybe the one feeds on the other?

'A family lives inside four walls and you should not knock them down if you want to have a house', claimed Pádraig. When I pushed him to elaborate on his reasons for being so apprehensive, he referred to one's pride: you have to have your pride. If he ever bought a car with borrowed money, he would not tell anyone. Maybe he would not be able to pay for it and then he would lose the car, and his pride too if more people had known about it! Seeing that I was not fully convinced by his argument, he then pointed to one of his neighbours, a man who has a field behind Pádraig's house and passes by every morning to check his cattle. He always glances into the house whenever he comes near on his way to the field. That is an awful habit, Pádraig thinks. 'They are always trying to suck information from you, and then when you might need them they might turn their back on you.' Did he mean that had they been more helpful when he needed them, he would have been more permissive with their nosy habits?

The circulation of information is integrated into a wider network of interhousehold mutual aid and services, in such a way that when information does not flow as it is expected, the whole circuit of reciprocal exchanges becomes blocked. 'Gossip is the commodity which is exchanged most in country life,' Emmett has written about a Welsh community; 'it is the currency of social relationships and the Llan man saves it up to help himself and his relatives' (1964: 117). The physical proximity that a small neighbourhood provides encourages the circulation of information: for obvious reasons, no gossip exchanges could be *possible* were people to live too far away from each other. But those exchanges can be *effective* as means of social control only as long as they participate in a wider circulation of reciprocities, in other words, as long as there is a specific social context that turns that physical proximity into a socially significant space.

Before concluding this chapter, we will have a look at the wider network of interhousehold reciprocities within which information exchanges seem to be so well integrated. It is not only on the farm that neighbours help each other; the running of the household in particular, and in more general terms, the multifarious circumstances of day-to-day interaction, all create a sphere of interhousehold social relationships, a network of symbolic and material exchanges as indefinite in content as are their encompassing neighbourhood boundaries. It is true, on the other hand, that the well-instituted patterns of neighbourhood interaction, as they were documented by Arensberg and Kimball (1937, [1940] 1968) and Hannan (1972), have long disappeared. People do not visit each other as often as they used to, and they all blame, almost unanimously, the television for this. Furthermore, some spheres of interhousehold exchanges at one time very common, such as the borrowing of groceries and even money, have been made redundant with the availability of cash provided by banks and other credit institutions, and also thanks to the availability of private cars, which have so drastically cut down the distance to the local shop of even the most isolated farmsteads.

Neighbourhood interaction has undoubtedly changed in the last few years; it has probably subsided to a great extent, but it has not yet disappeared altogether. Rites of passage, for instance, such as weddings and funerals, constitute a good occasion for the symbolic enactment of neighbourhood relations, sometimes also accompanied by material transactions, such as the presents offered at weddings, or the meals at wakes and funerals. Like relatives, neighbours are formally invited to weddings, and they are also expected to attend funerals and wakes, even though they are not formally invited except for the funeral meal. In the Three Districts, but not in other parishes as far as I could observe, the neighbours, not the relatives, are those who bury the dead since the latter are considered to be 'too close', too emotionally involved to carry out such a task.

In the same way as farm work exchanges and cooperation constitute an essentially male domain because of the gender bias of the farm and domestic worlds we have already seen, much of the extrafarm mutual aid between neighbours falls predominantly within the female sphere. My hostess Teresa Kelly and her neighbour Máire Maloney provide us with a good example. When Teresa had her third child, Máire used to come every day to give her a hand. She would stay there up to three or four hours, cleaning, vacuuming, bringing turf, preparing meals and, last but not least, having countless cups of tea and gossiping with Teresa. On another occasion, when Máire and her husband had to go to England for a funeral, Teresa kept Máire's four children until she came back, while her husband did the farm jobs for Máire's husband. The children of both families spend most of the time playing, and they can take their meals indistinctively in any of the houses (cf. Williams 1956: 143). Furthermore, since Máire has a driving licence and Teresa does not, lifts constitute another important service that Teresa can obtain from her neighbour.

I should remark on the fact that the husbands of these two women are foster brothers, so there is an additional relation that qualifies mere neighbourhood. But for the time being, I think we can set aside this supplementary bond, since much of what I could observe between those two households could be extrapolated to any other neighbourhood. It has to be pointed out that, in general terms, people show themselves in a very complimentary light when they refer to the good atmosphere they enjoy with their neighbours, despite the above-mentioned concern for the gossip dangers. Bridget McCann told me that her neighbours were very good when her daughter died; she remembered that all came to help, both herself in the house and her husband on the farm. She said that she visits most of them once a week, especially the old people who might need some help. For instance, she does the washing for two old bachelors, Paddy and Michael Carr, and her husband goes to play cards with them every Wednesday evening. 'Sometimes they might not want to see you very often,' another woman remarked. 'People like their privacy, you see, but they will run straightaway to see if any help is needed.' From what I could see, apart from the help offered on extraordinary occasions, such as deaths, accidents, illnesses, etc., the most common services that circulate within any neighbourhood are baby-sitting, especially among young mothers, lifts among drivers and nondrivers, and the general care of solitary elders, who have proliferated so rapidly in the last few years, even though this general care will never go as far as that given by kinfolk.

From the above discussion the reader can have a fair idea of the different social meanings encapsulated in the physical space of neighbourhood, of the different functions that rest upon the notion of physical distance. I corroborate that certainly a neighbour is not just the one who lives 'down there', but is also the person with whom we might have a row because his cattle broke into our field, the person who will keep an eye on us if we do not behave ourselves according to the expected standards, who might give us information we need about so-and-so, whose wife might baby-sit our children, from whom we might get a lift when needed, etc. Social conflict, social control and general social cooperation among neighbouring houses; all these spheres or transactional orders (Bloch and Parry 1989: 23ff) appear closely interrelated, in the same way as all of them are closely interrelated with the specific sphere of farm work reciprocities. The wider context within which farm work exchanges circulate turns out to be particularly complex.

13. INDIVIDUALISM, MORALITY, AND SENTIMENT

*F*amily, kinship and neighbourhood have turned the economic unit of the farm into a social institution; they have 'de-economised' the farm economy. As a result of this process, it could be argued that we are facing an economy that is less and less 'economic', so to speak. We will see now what theoretical consequences can be inferred from it. An economy that is no longer economic appears, certainly, as a logical contradiction. Is there any concept that can help us to come to terms with this blatant inconsistency? Is there any way we can think of a noneconomic economy? There is.

The concept of moral economy is not new in the social sciences. As it was analysed in Scott's seminal work (1976; cf. Thompson 1971), the concept of moral economy appeared as the theoretical antithesis of capitalism. It was the counterpart of individualism, selfishness and profit-maximising attitudes rediscovered in the communitarian and altruistic values of the preindustrial world. In fact, the very idea that the economy could be 'moral' explicitly contradicts the most fundamental characteristic of capitalist culture, which defines itself precisely as liberated from the jurisdiction of morals (Dumont 1977: 61–81).

Although 'moral economists' took great pains to sophisticate their arguments, they certainly insinuated the danger of a romantic idealisation of peasant societies that did not escape their critics. Shortly after the publication of Scott's study, Popkin retorted with another analysis of peasant politics in Southeast Asia with the very meaningful title of 'The Rational Peasant' (1979). Methodological individualism was substituted here for the 'moral economy approach' to peasant society. Theories of individual decision making and individual choice were used for the interpretation of peasant institutions in a fashion analogous to the analysis of ordinary market economies.

This controversy between 'moral' and 'political' economists was sparked by the necessity of making sense out of a very concrete historical situation – peasant insurgency in Southeast Asia. Still, it is clear to me that the general theoretical background upon which it developed has important implications for the conceptualisation of economic behaviour in a nonmarket context. For moral economists, economic action in peasant societies has a normative character; it has to be understood as the implementation of a moral rule with complete disregard for the interests of the individual, otherwise it will appear to us as utterly irrational. For political economists, in contrast, it is the primacy of the individual's interests and his strategically oriented behaviour that deserve the utmost attention – taking into account the important qualification that those individual interests include both economic and sociopolitical dividends.

None of these models in their most simplistic formulation – which, certainly, does not do full justice to their actual complexity – seemed to agree with my observations among western Irish farmers, especially with regard to their nonmarket economic relations. We have seen that the farming communities of the west of Ireland are deeply integrated into the world market economy, and they undoubtedly participate in the individualistic and profit-maximising ethos that characterises all capitalist societies, but they still have a substantial sphere of noncommodity transactions. It is in this domain of economic relations that neither the moral economy nor the political economy approach provides, in my view, an entirely satisfactory perspective.

Yet at the same time, both of them hint at important attributes of that sphere of noncommodity transactions. Farmers exchange all sorts of different services and products on a regular basis without taking any account of what is given in return. No customary regulation seems to govern this unsystematic flow of exchanges except a diffuse norm of generalised reciprocity. In the absence of explicit contractual agreements, there is a certain feeling of moral obligation that induces one to reciprocate the help that one has obtained. This feeling of moral obligation never seems to harden into a precise normative conduct, though. On the other hand, it would not be difficult to work out an underlying 'investment logic' in all those informal transactions, especially if we take a long-term perspective (Bloch 1973). But to look for surreptitious strategic attitudes behind an apparently normative or quasi-normative behaviour is always a tricky endeavour.[1]

In any case, by now it should be clear that on closer examination those unsystematic exchanges turn out to be less so. Generalised reciprocity always presupposes the existence of a social framework that sanctions the development of an otherwise arbitrary gift-giving. A first approach to the nature of this social framework in the farming communities of the west of Ireland can be almost syllogistically deduced from Sahlins's 'sociology of primitive exchange' (1972) and represented by a very simple model. By and large, farmers seem to cooperate informally only with people falling into at least two of the following categories: relatives, neighbours and farmers. That is to say, they will mainly cooperate with people who are either relatives and neighbours, relatives and farmers, neighbours and farmers or the three categories at the same time. The explanation runs as follows.

We know that this type of relationships, as opposed to contractual agreements, does not involve any fixed and predetermined form of payment. But what it certainly does involve, however, is an expectation that some form of counter-service will be performed in the long run. That is why a trust bond constitutes the basis of a relationship of generalised reciprocity. The question we have to answer now is how such expectation is created. A farmer can easily reciprocate the help he received from another farmer, since both are engaged in the same type of work, but two or more farmers will very rarely cooperate unless they also happen to be neighbours or relatives. It is easy to understand why. Were I to help a farmer who did not live in my neighbourhood I would have few possibilities of getting in return any assistance from him, since he would probably not travel too long a distance just to reciprocate my help. So the expectation of getting my return would be very low. Now, if the man is not my neighbour but happens to be my relative he might not travel that distance either, but there is already a circulation of reciprocal services between the two of us and our respective families: we exchange gifts at every rite of passage, we visit each other on Sunday afternoons, we might borrow money from each other, we might help each other in situations of family crisis, etc. Therefore, I can draw upon the already existing system of exchanges in order to 'get paid' for the help I offered. The expectation of getting my return is, consequently, higher.

---

1. This is an illegitimate transformation of the 'market metaphor' into a general theory of human action, according to a recent critic (Dilley 1992: 15ff).

But what would happen then if the man who is helping on my farm were a relative but not a farmer? There would already be a system of exchanges linking the two of us as kin or affines. But that would not suffice to guarantee that I would have enough opportunities to return the help I was getting from him *on my farm*. He would have then a low expectation of having his help reciprocated, unless there was something more to it: unless he was a neighbour too. Similar to kinship, neighbourhood provides another system of off-farm reciprocal exchanges: baby-sitting services, lifts to town, any type of domestic assistance, visiting, etc. Therefore, the combination of those two systems of reciprocities, those involved in kinship and those involved in neighbourhood, increases the likelihood that the help I got from my neighbouring relative on my farm can be reciprocated.

It is apparent from the above discussion that the farm provides a space for reciprocal exchanges and social interaction. But this space can only be operative, as far as relations of generalised reciprocity are concerned, if it acts in combination with other two similar spaces, neighbourhood and kinship. Left on its own, that is to say, without the complement of those two sets of social relations, the farm would lose much of its social character; it would become a purely economic entity that could relate to its subjects only through contractual agreements, the same as any other capitalist business. Conversely, kinship and neighbourhood provide a social space for a particular type of economic activity: farm work. But they can only be operative, as far as that economic activity is concerned, if they act in combination with each other, or in combination with the space provided by the farm itself. Alone, they would lose much of their economic significance, as happens with kinship and neighbourhood in the rest of capitalist society.

Underlying the capacity of the farm to assimilate, so to speak, different sets of social relations, there is the propensity of farm labour to circulate within social spheres that we would not normally associate with the economy. In so doing, the economic nature of farm work seems to become more and more confused into different orders of noneconomic transactions and, at the same time, those noneconomic transactions become generously pervaded by a certain sense of economic logic. This ambiguity, in the last instance, turns the farm into the meeting point of different types of 'rationalities', economic or otherwise. As Mendras has argued, 'on the family farm everything is both social and economic, and purchases of a tractor, a refrigerator, or a washing machine are all made according to the same procedure, allowing no opportunity for the economist to impose his point of view.' (1970: 87).

This de-economisation of farm work also has another significant consequence: it enables the farm to absorb and to become fused into the cultural specificity of its social milieu. Even though the model I have just outlined has been couched in very abstract terms, it is important to note that the relevance of kinship and neighbourhood as social frameworks for a specific set of productive relations cannot be taken as a universal fact. On the contrary, it is widely accepted that the so-called 'amoral familism' of rural societies foils in other cultural contexts the possibility of cooperative links between unrelated neighbours (Banfield 1958; Campbell 1964) – despite the strong theoretical and methodological criticism that such a concept has received (Silverman 1968). And similarly, kinship and affinity do not always suit the implementation of economic functions, as Ott has observed among Basque shepherds (1981: 61; cf. Abrahams 1984: 114–15).

The above model has very little meaning unless we relate it to the particular cultural features of western Irish farmers. Thus, the principle of unigeniture with reference to the inheritance of the family agricultural land, coupled with the widespread practice of offering a building site to noninheriting children, gives rise to the proliferation of what we could call 'extended family neighbourhoods': a farmer is very likely to have some of his brothers' or sisters' nonfarming families living nearby. Hence the overlapping of kinship and neighbourhood is not merely a coincidence but the result of a distinctive inheritance practice. Similarly, a remarkable pattern of local exogamy combined with occupational endogamy – farmers usually marry farmers' daughters from other parishes – extends affinity bonds beyond the limit of one's vicinity, so that the existence of those affinity bonds in non-neighbouring farmers appears in this case as the outcome of a specific marriage custom.

A case study will help us put a bit of flesh and blood into this somewhat arid discussion. But first, it is worth having a closer look at the meaning of kinship and neighbourhood in their role of social frameworks for the farm economy.

The possibility that kinship and neighbourhood might fulfil this particular function stems directly from their capacity to constitute themselves as moral universes. It is from this 'moralistic' point of view that the sphere of transactions distinctive of those two social domains cannot be too hastily subsumed under an investment or profit-maximising logic. Within one's kindred or neighbourhood there is a specific set of rights and obligations that does not apply to outsiders. This is what Fortes defined as 'amity' or 'prescriptive altruism' for the kinship sphere (1969: 219–49), although he explicitly referred to its possible extension to neighbourhood relationships (pp. 242–45). Following Young and Will-mott's study of east London (1986), Fortes explained this moral charac-ter in terms of the ascriptive character of kinship bonds (p. 242). Because I do not relate to my kin of my own volition but simply because they are my kin, we can have full confidence in each other since we are not linked by any particular interest; our relationship is beyond our will.[2]

Let us see now the qualities of these moral universes as regards their respective 'spheres of exchange'. According to Gell's recent critical revi-sion of the classical theory of generalised reciprocity (1992), we should not understand the exchanges that take place between people linked with moral bonds as 'reciprocal'. 'For instance, the provision of children by parents', he argues, 'involves material transfers which flow directly form the moral definition of role-relationships between parents and children, and not "prestations" which produce or repay "debts".' (Gell 1992: 152).

It seems to me, however, that the difference between Gell's views and Sahlins's concept of generalised reciprocity is less sharp than it might appear. We could establish a scale that would go from 'pure' contractual relationships, including both monetary exchanges and barter, to 'pure' moral links. At one extreme we would have all those exchanges that do not entail any moral bond between the parties; monetary transactions would figure prominently among them.[3] Somewhere in the middle we would find all the different gradations of 'reciprocal exchanges' in which some feeling of delayed returns is not entirely absent, so that they can-not be understood as merely the result of a moral duty; but at the same

---

2. It is true, on the other hand, that Fortes, and anthropological theory of kinship in general terms, defines the specificity of the kinship bond in opposition to affinity. The extent to which affinity stems out of a marriage contract seems to exclude it from the sphere of ascriptive relationships. It should be noted, however, that this contractual character affects the link between husband and wife, but it appears as much less definitive with regard to the relationships of each partner with his/her respective in-laws. The fact that I relate to my in-laws has to be explained in terms of the kinship – and therefore ascriptive – bond that links them to my wife, despite the contractual nature of the marriage bond that links the two of us. Furthermore, the affective content encapsulated in a marriage bond sets it quite apart from any other form of ordinary contractual relationship. I shall return to this later (cf. Schnei-der 1968: 76ff).

3. See Macfarlane's analysis of the 'amoral' character of money as 'the root of all evil' (1987: 98–122; cf. Bloch and Parry 1989: 17–19).

time, the parties are not entitled to offer their services in the expectation that they are going to be reciprocated (Pitt-Rivers 1971: 139), so there is in them some sense of moral obligation as well. Finally, at the other extreme we would have those transactions that take place simply as the implementation of moral responsibilities and for which no counter-service is in any form envisaged.[4] Therefore, the degree to which a specific service is offered with some expectation of reciprocity, or the degree to which it is offered out of a moral obligation, would help us place each particular transaction between the two poles of the scale, closer to one extreme or closer to the other.

Gell's radical distinction between morality and reciprocity is useful, but it may also be misleading. We can see a different point of view in the observations made by Gudeman and Rivera in their analysis of the Colombian peasantry: 'The trade [of work] is set within broader social relationships. Because it is a delayed transaction, a loan to be repaid, the exchange must be underwritten by confidence and trust. Labor trade is always undertaken with neighbors, kin, or friends, for it is said that one can have little confidence in a stranger.' But why is there little confidence in a stranger? Why is labour trade always undertaken with particular categories of individuals? 'There are few inducements to underperform in the trade of labor,' Gudeman and Rivera add, 'because a person receives back what he has given, and the enduring bonds of which the transaction is a part allow social sanctions to have full effect' (1990: 110). Those enduring bonds are in turn integrated by specific sets of transactions, in such a way that the failure to comply with one's moral obligations, or to fulfil the other's expectations, can be penalised not with the lack of repayment but with the disruption of the flow of exchanges characteristic of each of those sets. In my view, this penalisation does not challenge the moral character of those transactions, it simply shows that a moral obligation cannot be too drastically isolated from its material implications, or at least, not under any circumstance.

4. Here we come across Pitt-Rivers's distinction between structurally stressed and unstressed kin (1973: 103). Commenting, precisely, on Fortes's ideas about the jural and moral aspects of kinship, Pitt-Rivers maintained that purely moral services, devoid of any sense of debt or repayment, could be transacted only between structurally unstressed kin, since only in this case is their relationship of pure 'amity', free from the jural aspects that conform to the relationships between the other type of kin. It should be emphasised, on the other hand, that Pitt-Rivers included the affines within his category of structurally unstressed kin, whereas Fortes had explicitly excluded them from his axiom of amity (1969: 234–35).

Let me summarise the arguments that have been put forward thus far. The present discussion has to be understood as a problematisation of the concept of moral economy as regards the particular mode of production of western Irish farmers. My first point was that the definition of kinship and neighbourhood as moral universes precludes us from a simplistic application of an individualistic methodology. The investment logic characteristic of market transactions cannot be extrapolated to other social spheres, because in so doing we overlook the distinctive social framework incorporated by their specific system of exchanges. But at the same time, I have argued that there is a material basis for those moral universes, that there are material consequences derived from the implementation or failure to implement their idiosyncratic 'prescriptive altruism', and that these material consequences result from the flow of material exchanges that circulate within their respective spheres.

The morality of kinship and neighbourhood that we have seen in operation among the family farmers of the west of Ireland is of a very special sort; it is far from having the universalistic character that, according to social philosophers, should distinguish all moral precepts.[5] Unlike what we will see in the next chapter, the morality of kinship and neighbourhood incorporates a set of rights and obligations that are projected upon a restricted category of people. It is not everybody that becomes indebted to me when I help my neighbour or kin but only my neighbour or kin. And I do help him precisely because he is my neighbour or kin, that is to say, he belongs to a category of people with whom I am supposed to be related by a myriad of different transactions. So this is not so much 'prescriptive altruism' as 'selective altruism'.

On the other hand, the moral feeling that undoubtedly permeates transactions between neighbours or kin has a very apparent material dimension that somehow reminds us of the relevance of individual interests, that somehow evokes a disguised 'investment logic'. But to reduce it to a mere long-term maximising rationality appears to me as a cunning simplification that misses important elements of human experience. In what follows I will present a very brief case study that will illustrate some of the points that have already been developed and enlarge them into a somewhat different dimension. Perhaps the dramatic intensity of an ordinary event might help reformulate more clearly meandering theoretical predicaments.

---

5. Cf. Campbell's assertion that the values of honour and prestige among the Sarakatsani 'have a moral content of their own but they cannot be referred to any universal moral principle' (1964: 317).

This case study was recorded during the hay harvest of the summer of 1990. The hay harvest is such an important event in the farming communities of the west of Ireland that it really seems as if making hay is what farming is all about to them. As has already been suggested, the hay harvest turns out to be a catalyst for social engagements of unparalleled intensity and transcendence. For the hay harvest, anyone who happens to be around will be recruited: farmers and nonfarmers, men and women, children and elders, neighbours, relatives, strangers, anthropologists – all are thrown into the hay field. It seems to me that the hay harvest can be taken as a kind of synecdoche of the social world of the farming communities of the west of Ireland, a singular event endowed with the strange capacity to materialise in a few weeks, maybe in a few days, all the intricacies of a particular social structure.

In the summer of 1990, the hay harvest of my neighbour Joe Maloney validated in the apparent simplicity of a prosaic episode the complexity of all those cross-cutting connotations. Joe is a full-time farmer with forty-five acres of land; he is married and has four children aged between twelve and three. For the hay he usually gets the help of his friend and next-door neighbour Seán Rabbitte, a young bachelor and part-time farmer. That summer, however, Seán was not available. The weather had been very good thus far, but heavy showers in a few days had been forecast, so everybody in the parish was suffering from 'hay madness'. Networks of reciprocity were put to their limit; some of them were broken, some new ones were created. To save the hay was the top priority at the time, at whatever cost.

But Joe found himself collecting the bales on his own, with the help only of his wife and eldest son. To pick up bales of hay is a tough job; they have to be lifted with a fork and thrown into a trailer, where somebody has to build them up. Even though Joe's wife and the child were doing their best, the work was advancing very slowly, much to Joe's distress. In the meantime, Pádraig Kelly, Joe's foster brother who also happens to live just a few yards from him, was coming home from work at half past five every evening without paying too much attention to his neighbour's sufferings, and not entirely because he is not fond of farm work. Pádraig is a factory worker, married as well with three little children, and reared on the same family farm as Joe. Enthusiastic as he always was for the things of the farm, he inherited only a building site from his foster father; Joe got the farm. Very bitter feelings have arisen between the two men ever since.

Despite this bad relationship between Joe and Pádraig, their respective wives, Máire and Teresa, get along extremely well (we met them in

Chapter 12). They baby-sit for each other now and again and have many cups of tea together every day. While Máire has a driving licence, Teresa does not, so the latter gets lifts from the other whenever she wants; this is very important in isolated settlements. Maybe it was this well-established relation of good friendship and domestic reciprocities that triggered the concern of Pádraig's wife for what was going on. 'It is a sin to see our neighbours killing themselves at the fields and not give them any help', she would repeat now and again, with no positive answer from Pádraig. But sometimes she would adopt a more conciliatory tone: 'And then again we are not farmers, you see, we are independent and we owe nothing to them. It's time for them to do a bit of work, all year round sitting back while we are working every day!' In any case, whatever changes of mood she might show (probably just a device to get around Pádraig's assertive patriarchalism), she was perfectly aware of her increasingly delicate situation. She had become the precarious link between two antagonistic moral universes: her husband's and her friend's husband's.

It was a fragile tie that was about to break if those moral universes fell too violently apart. The following Saturday the two women were supposed to go to Mass together. Teresa phoned her neighbour to ask her about it, but one of Máire's sons said that she was not in. 'But she must be in since the car is at the door', Teresa observed. That Saturday, Máire was not going to give her any lift. Whatever the true reason, it is important to note her own personal interpretation: 'That's it, see, we didn't help them for the hay, now I couldn't go to Mass.' In her understanding of the situation, there was a unique circuit of reciprocities linking the two households wherein farm labour, domestic services, friendship and neighbourhood relationships of whatever kind all mixed together and were mutually exchangeable, in such a way that the breaking of that circuit at any of its components, farm labour in this case, would inevitably stop the normal flow of the rest.

Fortunately, the ill-feelings did not go all that far. The next day Joe realised that he could not manage only with the help of his wife and son, so he decided to ask Pádraig explicitly for help. Confronted by his foster brother's explicit request, Pádraig could not refuse if he really did not want to provoke a very serious estrangement between the two of them. He was even thinking of taking a day off from the factory to work with Joe. In a few days he would have his summer holidays and he would certainly not feel like working then: 'When you are at home all day you cannot avoid helping.' So for the following three days Pádraig went to the hay field as soon as he came home from the factory, and an immediate reactivation of the circulation of reciprocities between the two house-holds ensued. While the two men were working together with the help of Joe's wife, Teresa baby-sat the small children for the two families. (Previously they had been with the old couple, Joe and Pádraig's foster parents.) Furthermore, on Wednesday, when the women of the parish usually go to bingo, the two women went together in Máire's car.

That was, once again, the social framework of the farm economy in operation. Let us have a quick glimpse of the radiography of this social framework. At this concrete level, it certainly turns out to be slightly more complex than it looked in the abstract model. We have, on the one hand, relations of good neighbourliness qualified by a loose bond of fic-tive kinship (fosterage) linking the two men, Joe and Pádraig. On the other, we have the same relation of good neighbourhood coupled with an even looser tie of what we could define as 'fictive affinity' linking the two women, Máire and Teresa. In both these situations we could claim that there is a certain feeling of moral duty derived from the intersection of two sets of social relations, kinship and neighbourhood – two sets of social relations that should also be understood as moral universes. But it is a moral duty that incorporates very different emotional contents and, furthermore, a difference that seems to be inversely correlated with the presence of the (fictive) kinship bond. Máire and Teresa, only fictively affines, keep on good terms, whereas Joe and Pádraig, foster brothers, have a very cool relationship. This emotional dimension, on the other hand, is even more apparent in the tie that, in turn, links the two men with the two women: marriage. It is because Teresa is married to Pádraig and Máire to Joe that the contingencies of the relationship between the two foster brothers reverberate on the set of reciprocities linking the two women: Máire did not get her lift because her husband did not help Joe.

It could be argued from the above that the economic relation that enabled Joe to save his hay has an undeniable moral nature. But to under-stand this economic relation as an instance of a moral economy should not make us overlook the capacity of such a relation to act as an 'emo-tional container', because, in the last instance, that emotional content decisively determined the actual possibility of the economic transaction between the two foster brothers. Pádraig was under a moral obligation to help Joe with the hay harvest. But the bitter feelings that existed between the two men, which prevented Pádraig from giving a hand to his foster brother in the first place, cannot be deduced from that moral duty. I have suggested that Pádraig's disinheritance from the family land has certainly contributed to that animosity. But in a system of unigeniture, such as that prevailing in the west of Ireland, there is disinheritance from the family land at every generational replacement, which does not necessarily lead to the breakdown of all relationships between siblings! In other words, I am suggesting that the hostility between the two foster brothers cannot be understood without considering the emotional side of all long-standing and intimate relationships. It is a hostility that, interestingly, was always explained to me in terms of the lack of a blood tie.

On the other hand, we could cynically claim that the pressure exercised by Máire on her husband, although couched in a moral language ('It is a sin to see our neighbours killing themselves at the fields and not give them any help'), was in fact motivated by her interest in maintaining a good relationship with Joe's wife. But why did Pádraig give in to his wife's persuasion? Because he did not want to strain the stability of his own marriage by putting at risk his wife's friendship with Máire? Because he eventually felt the moral duty that obliges him to help his neighbour and foster brother? Or maybe the moral duty that compels him to keep his wife happy no matter what? Again, we realise that the dichotomy normative/strategical does not exhaust all the possibilities of human behaviour.

This dichotomy normative/strategical reverberates in other well-established oppositions in anthropological thought that are now being put into question: contract/status, gift/commodities, community/association, individualism/collectivism, etc. All of them, to some extent, are derived from the now much-criticised discrimination between primitives and moderns. In what way does the present discussion help overcome such time-honoured polarities? In the foregoing account I have been emphasising the importance of the emotional side in the social relationships under study. It is not my intention to vindicate the need for introducing some form of psychological bias into the analysis of social relationships, but merely to open the space for a deeper (sociological) understanding of the economic behaviour we have been examining in the previous paragraphs.

There is, we could claim, a sphere of transactions, or a sphere of human behaviour in general terms, that cannot be subsumed either to an individualistic profit-maximising rationality or to a collectivistic normative logic. This is what we could loosely define as the domain of the emotional, radically distinguished from the principles of economic rationality but, at the same time, with an indisputable individualistic imprint that sets it well apart from any moral or normative sphere.[6] Nothing ter-

---

6. Cf. Cheal's opposition between 'structures of community' and 'structures of intimacy' in his theory of gift-giving in modern societies (1988: 169ff).

ribly original has been said so far. That human beings can be sentimental, in the same way as they are rational and moral, should be no surprise to anyone. The important point to stress here is not the suitability of a psychology of emotions to make sense of this 'sentimental logic', but the existence of a particular *social structure* that turns personal sentiments into socially relevant attitudes. In this case, those personal sentiments turn out to be not just socially but *economically* relevant, since they form a constitutive ingredient of a specific set of productive relations.

14. WORK AS METAPHOR
The Abrogation of the Economy

We already know in what sense the moral economy of Irish farmers can be understood as a 'sentimental economy', so I could conclude my argument here. But there is still one last point that deserves further development. The fact that kinship and, to a lesser extent, neighbourhood operate as emotional containers does not entirely erase their nature of moral communities, even though this moral character is profoundly distorted by the powerful influence of personal sentiments. Let us now leave this sphere of emotions and let us concentrate on the concept of morality.

An economy that defines itself as a moral economy certainly includes the negation of itself. It is an economy ruled by an external normative body that, by definition, cannot be modelled according to an economistic ethos, otherwise it would not be external. When this external normative body is provided by kinship and neighbourhood, however, the negation of the economy is only partial. Because kinship and neighbourhood are only partially external to the farm economy, they are only partially 'moral'. Each with its own sphere of exchange, they both participate in the farm economy in such a way that the moral framework they provide in the short term can be recast as rational-individualistic strategy in the long term. In other words, kinship and neighbourhood have a *syntagmatic* relationship to the farm economy. Consequently, if we are to find a pure instance of moral economy in the Three Districts we have to get away from kinship and neighbourhood. We have to look for a sphere of exchanges that in no way can be seen as part of the farm economy, neither in the short term nor in the long term. We have to look for a normative body not with a syntagmatic but with a *paradigmatic* relationship to the farm economy.

The principle by which I have defined the 'most economic' relations of this community, the contractual principle, stems from the wider notion of reciprocity, which is probably one of the most elementary rules of any type of social formation (Gouldner 1960). But how far can this notion of reciprocity actually be pushed? In the next paragraphs we will use the concept of reciprocity in a cultural domain that could not be more at odds with the ideology of economic exchanges. We will jump into a sphere of transactions that, to follow Bloch and Parry (1989: 24), brings us near to the long-term reproduction of the 'cosmic' order. The analysis of the very concept of work now leads us to a further enquiry. This will, however, take us in a rather unexpected direction.

When I returned with one of my Irish friends from my first ascent to the holy mountain of Croagh Patrick, in Co. Mayo, his wife told me that she would not have been able to do it. 'You have no brains for it', her husband reproached her. 'You don't need brains for that!' she replied, slightly irritated. After a while, she commented to me jokingly that I should get a good job when I went back home after all the penance I had gone through. On another occasion, a middle-aged farm woman told me that she had climbed the holy mountain barefooted three times. It was as a thanksgiving for a promise she had made. The last time, she thought she would put on her boots because she felt very tired, but one of the straps broke as she was going to tie it. She interpreted that as a sign that she had to go with her feet bare once again. So she did, and she said to me proudly that she had only minor problems on her feet after the climb, as if suggesting that they were somehow protected by the holiness of her enterprise.

Declan Kennedy remembers that he once saw a man in Croagh Patrick going around the chapel at the top on his knees. That was a really tough penance. It could have been as a thanksgiving for something you already had, he explained, as a way of enforcing your petitions, or just for the redemption of your sins. 'Say if a neighbour was sick, you would pray for him and do some penance.' Your petitions do not go directly to God, but to the Holy Virgin or to the saints, who are the intermediaries between human beings and God. In any case, you had better accompany them with some form of suffering. Confronted by my impertinent scepticism, my friend courteously elaborated on his ideas: 'I might be living

according to the law of God, I do no harm to anybody, but my neighbour is having some trouble. I can pray for him, you see, but if I fast or
I do penance my prayers get more powerful, like. It is like everything else,
you have to concentrate on what you are doing. If you are talking to me
and then I go to watch the cattle you will think that I have very bad man-
ners, that I am not listening to you. The same when I am talking to God
… That's the Catholic belief anyhow, you have to suffer if you want
something from God.' There was a priest in the church some years
before, Declan said to me on another occasion, a man with curative pow-
ers, a very holy man. 'Lots of people can tell you that, but very few knew
the awful penances he was going through. Once, somebody went to see
him on a frosty night in the winter, and he was walking around the
church barefooted! It is not easy to walk barefooted on the frost!'

Penance is suffering, in whatever way that suffering is achieved, on
the only condition that it has to be, apparently, fruitless; it has to be for
its own sake. The pains endured by a mother delivering a baby are not
penance, nor is the suffering of the farmer feeding the stock on a cold
and rainy winter morning, not even that of a man who is helping a sick
neighbour and is not expecting anything in return. Suffering should
arise as an end in itself and not as a means to obtain something else, no
matter how laudable that something else might be.

Fasting, abstinence and penance in general terms all constitute practices characteristic not only of Catholicism but of many other religions.
But it seems that in Irish Catholicism they have always been particularly
prominent. As Russell has pointed out, 'the association of physical
denial, sacred power and the status of "holy person" represents a pervasive motif in Irish religiosity' (1979: 171–72). There is a widespread
interpretation of those practices that associates them with the masochis-
tic excesses of penitential zeal stemming from Celtic religious traditions
(referred to by Brown 1985: 20; see also Danaher 1972: 54–57 and
Scheper-Hughes 1979: 219, n. 11). More sociologically minded scholars, on the other hand, tend to privilege their functional implications at
the expense of their historical origins: 'Engagement in these practices
was undoubtedly part of the overall struggle to attain social prestige by
appearing to be morally superior' (Inglis 1987: 131). I will come back
to this later.

I would suggest that for a correct interpretation of penance we should
think about it in a wider network of reciprocal exchanges, both symbolic
and material, which call upon religious institutions for their implementation. The church, first of all, centralises and gives expression to certain

types of services and counter-services that circulate within the community itself. A good example of it is the celebration of Masses. If I have received a very important favour or service from another person, something that I might not be able to reciprocate due to its extraordinary nature -e.g., a blood transfusion that saved my life – I can show my gratitude by paying for a Mass for the person from whom I got that favour. Similarly, on the occasion of a funeral, friends and relatives of the deceased buy Mass cards and offer them to the bereaved family as a token of solidarity and empathy with their sorrow. Each card stands for a Mass to be celebrated for the soul of the deceased person. Sometimes it is money that is given directly. I remember when I attended a funeral at the end of the service the bereaved family stood at the door of the church collecting money from those coming out.[1] Again, it was supposed to be offered to the church for the celebration of Masses for the deceased person's soul.

In all these examples, the church acts as a broker between the two parties involved in a reciprocal exchange, its system of meanings providing an adequate code for the expression of symbolic counter-services. There are other instances, however, in which reciprocal exchange does not take place among the members of the community but between God and a particular individual. When that is the case, the brokerage of the church is more indirect. It still provides its system of meanings, but now there is no material reward accruing to the church. The relation of exchange takes place only between God and the individual, usually through the mediation of minor supernatural entities such as the Holy Virgin or the saints. Sometimes priests can also intervene as further intermediaries between those supernatural entities and the lay subject, but not necessarily, and, in any case, this mediation is of a different nature from that which we saw earlier.

As a member of the Catholic Church I am liable to some duties, such as going to Mass, confession, rites of passage, fasting, etc. It could be said that to comply with those prescriptions does not entitle me to any special grace from God, but special misfortunes might happen to me if I do not go through with them. A mother of three children who had not been to Mass for a few weeks told me once, in a very distressed state, that she would do her best not to miss Mass the next Sunday; she was afraid that something might happen to the children if she did not go. So a certain relation of exchange is already established by the very performance of

1. Cf. the 'offerings' documented by Kane in Donegal (1968: 249–50).

those rituals, a relation of exchange in which a sort of general protection against misfortunes can be considered as the counter-service obtained. More clearly, however, since my church membership does not oblige me to go through extraordinary penances such as climbing the holy mountain of Croagh Patrick barefoot, I am more than likely to be entitled to special assistance from God, parallel to the special nature of the service I have offered.

But the existence of an exchange relation is not as straightforward. Most people who do penances on the one hand and claim to have been helped by God on the other, do not always establish a causal link between the two.[2] They argue that they go through penance because they are good Catholics, because that is the Catholic belief, and they point to an imprecise connection between penance and the possibility that your prayers can be more effective, but they hardly ever support the existence of a *quid pro quo* relation between penance and God's help. Does this mean that penances and supernatural favours do not participate in the same circuit of exchanges?

I do not think so. What it means, in my view, is that they are not linked by a contractual relation, or by a 'symbolic' contractual relation, that is to say, a relation involving predefined counter-services, but by a relation of generalised reciprocity, in which the terms of exchange are left to the free will of the parties, so to speak, on the understanding, certainly, that some sort of balance will be struck in the long term.[3] As we have seen in the previous chapters, people who engage in relations of generalised reciprocity with their neighbours or kin always argue that they cooperate with them as a sign of 'good neighbourliness', or because you are supposed to help your kinfolk, but they never explain their offer of help in terms of the counter-services they might obtain in exchange, even though they do not deny that there is an expectation of receiving some form of counter-service sooner or later. This is precisely the same type of argument put forward by penitents. A man helps his neighbours

2. In his analysis of the Lough Derg pilgrimage, Victor Turner (1978: ch. 3) refutes the idea that pilgrims look for 'material favours' in exchange for the ordeal they have to go through. He prefers instead to define Lough Derg as just a place of worship and 'spiritual' penance (p. 129). Some counter-evidence has been documented by Russell, though, who maintains that the reasons for penance in Lough Derg are, according to the penitents themselves, to get rid of illnesses, either affecting the penitent or another person close to him, or to get a job, to get a husband or a wife, etc. (1978: 238–40). Maybe what Turner should have clarified is what he meant by 'material favours'.

3. Foster (1963) uses his concept of 'dyadic contract' to understand the patron-client relationships he observed between supernatural beings and Catholic peasants

or kin *because* they are neighbours or kin, in the same way as a penitent goes through some form of ordeal *because* he is a good Catholic. This does not mean that there is no expectation of returns; it simply means that such expectation cannot be taken as a justification of the initial offer, which takes place on the basis, I insist, not of the counter-service expected, but on the basis of a preexisting social relation, be this neighbourhood, kinship, or religion.

That reciprocal exchanges with the supernatural constitute one of the most elementary forms of exchange was pointed out long ago by Marcel Mauss in his masterpiece on the gift:

> One of the first groups of beings with which men had to enter into contract, and who, by definition, were there to make a contract with them, were above all the spirits of both the dead and of the gods. Indeed, it is they who are the true owners of the things and possessions of this world. With them it was most necessary to exchange, and with them it was most dangerous not to exchange. Yet conversely, it was with them it was easiest and safest to exchange. The purpose of destruction by sacrifice is precisely that it is an act of giving that is necessarily reciprocated ([1950] 1990: 16).

Mauss is using here the word 'contract' in a much wider sense than the restricted one I have been employing myself, but in any case I think that his understanding of sacrifice goes hand in hand with my interpretation of penitential practices. In fact, penance is no more than a form of self-sacrifice.[4] From this the transactional nature of penance, its power

---

in a Mexican village, very similar to those I am documenting in this chapter. Interestingly, however, even though he remarks on the existence of what he calls 'continuing patron-client relationships', which fit in quite well with my model of generalised reciprocity, he also accounts for 'non-continuing, short term contracts', with clearly predefined returns. In these, people would comply with their promises (for what he says, not always involving penance) only on condition that they get what they asked for, and if they do not, he even reports on ways of 'punishing' the saint, such as turning his picture to the wall or placing it face down on a chair (p. 1290; see also Pina-Cabral 1986: 163ff).

4. This seems to contradict the 'the communication theory' of sacrifice, the former theory held by Hubert and Mauss ([1898] 1964). But as Bloch has recently argued, Hubert and Mauss's dismissal of the gift theory of sacrifice is unsatisfactory, 'giving something is the lowest common denominator of rituals which have been called sacrifice, perhaps simply because this is a fundamental meaning of the word in modern European languages' (Bloch 1992: 30). It is worth pointing out, on the other hand, that Hubert and Mauss's interest in the identification of the sacrificer with the victim, as stressed by Bloch, appears most clearly precisely in the case of penance.

to act as a currency in exchanges with the supernatural, appears quite clearly. But there is another more intricate question we should try to answer now. Why does penance in particular have to be the currency used in those exchanges? Where does such necessity of physical denial stem from? In other words, why do we have to suffer if we want something from God and, above all, why such an apparently pointless suffering?

If the aim is to please God so that we might be entitled to receive his assistance when needed, one would have thought that God would be far more pleased were we to help a sick neighbour, for instance, rather than to engage ourselves in some tortuous ordeal out of which nobody is going to gain any profit. But maybe the aim is not so much to 'please' God as to create a *debt relation* with him, which is a different thing altogether. If I am helping a sick neighbour, even though I am not expecting anything in return, by the very fact of offering my help I am making him indebted to me; no matter how pleased God might be because of my good behaviour, it is not God who becomes indebted to me but my neighbour. Let us take the example of a man collecting bales of hay, all day long under a boiling sun but also under the threat of a forecast shower: all his muscles are working at full swing, his body is pouring sweat, he is anxious to finish his work as soon as possible, he is exhausted, he is suffering. If he happens to be working in his own meadow, his suffering is automatically compensated, so to speak, by the immediate profits he is going to get out of it: the saving of his hay harvest. But if he is working in his neighbour's meadow on the basis of a relation of generalised reciprocity, there is no immediate compensation for his suffering, no immediate repayment for his work, and it is precisely because of this that his neighbour will get into debt to him. In other words, the debt arises out of unpaid work. And if we define work, in opposition to leisure, as an activity that is never an end in itself but a means to achieve something else – payment – unpaid work looks very much like 'pointless' work, as pointless as the most severe of penances.

The person who wants God indebted to him faces the following dilemma: if he works for himself, nobody is indebted to him but himself; if he works for somebody else for no payment, it is the third person for whom he is working who is going to be indebted to him; if he does not work, no debt is created, because it is unpaid work that creates a debt. But how can I work for no payment and at the same time for no one, not even for myself? What I need is a type of activity that looks very much like work without being work, because, let us say it again, work can never be an end in itself but a means to achieve something

144

else. Suffering is an activity that has the essential characteristic of work, but out of which nobody is going to get any benefit. What I need is not work but a *metaphor* of work. And here is where penance, that pointless suffering (pointless work) fulfils its role.

Penance is symbolic work to put into debt the most symbolic of all beings: God. And if Durkheim told us that God is a symbol that stands for human society, we could argue that it is eventually human society that becomes indebted to us through our symbolic work. Would that be the origin of the 'social prestige' that accrues for the penitents, according to Inglis? Religious identity is an inescapable requisite for community membership in the Three Districts. Only those who for whatever reason cannot be seen as belonging to the community, such as the commuters with no connections with the local farming families (see Chapter 12), or myself, a total stranger, can escape from the compulsiveness of religious duties. But if a 'local' decided not to attend Mass any more, or explicitly disavowed religious prescriptions, such as fasting during Lent, etc., he would be the object of talk among neighbours. It would not be as bad as in the 'old days', people immediately recognise, when those who did not go to Mass were denounced at the missions, or the parish priest read aloud the names and contributions of the parishioners to the parish fund. Still, the religious rebel would be accused of being 'Protestant' or 'odd', and sooner or later he would suffer a certain emotional ostracism that would certainly hamper his social activities and relations. I remember when on Ash Wednesday evening I went to the bingo game with the women of the parish. They started to talk about their fasting exercises, about what they would not eat or drink, about their cravings for cigarettes when they had decided not to smoke during Lent; it seemed to me that anyone who had not been able to reveal her private 'ordeal' would have been inevitably marginalised from the conversation. Even I myself was defined, half jokingly, as 'very holy' because I had gone twice to Croagh Patrick!

My aim in relating the above anecdotes is to demonstrate how exquisite is the mechanism by which religious practices confer moral prestige to their adherents, in particular, those practices that involve some form of suffering, either through abstinence or any other type of penance. The community holds in high regard those individuals who are ready to suffer for the sake of their beliefs: these are the 'holy people'. It is important to emphasise that the logic of those practices and their social implications cannot be understood without the mediation of God. By rights, it is God and only God who becomes indebted to the penitent, and not one's neighbours, kin or fellow farmers. And it is only when God is seen as the symbolic mediator for human society that the indebtedness to God is somehow transferred to one's fellow human beings in terms of moral prestige.

But what is the nature of the paradigmatic relationship of religious practices with the material world of the farm economy? The utmost expression of a moral entity in the west of Ireland still is the Catholic church. Only those who comply with its prescriptions can partake of its moral credentials, because only they belong to the Catholic Church as another moral community. But the relationship between the moral credentials obtained from the performance of religious duties and the farm economy is only indirect, and indirect in a double sense. It is indirect because the Catholic practitioner acquires moral prestige by putting God, rather than his neighbour or kin, into debt. Only because God stands as a symbol for human society can we say that fellow human beings, who also have a relationship to God, are indebted to us. It is an indirect debt, mediated through God. Furthermore, it is indirect in a second sense since that distinctive type of moral prestige only becomes relevant to the farm economy to the extent that it impinges upon a particular group of people: those who happen to fall into any one of the particular moral communities we have seen before, kinship and neighbourhood. In other words, to the extent that the farm economy is seen as embedded in wider fields of social interaction. Still, no matter how indirectly, and no matter how much religious consciousness has declined in the west of Ireland, very little social interaction takes place outside the moral universe provided by the Catholic Church.

If we try to think about penance in the context of the previous analysis, that is to say, to think about penance as a metaphoric work in the context of our analysis of work relationships, we can see how work acquires an increasing moral character in the process of losing its economic nature. When work was exchanged under a contractual agreement, that moral character was virtually nonexistent since the parties were supposed to belong to different 'moral communities'. When it was exchanged in virtue of a relation of generalised reciprocity with a particular set of human subjects, work acquired a double-sided constitution: half economic and half moral. Economic, because it was still expected to provide material benefits although only in the long term; moral, because the short-term motivation for the exchange was the feeling of moral duty that binds all the subjects belonging to a particular moral community, neighbourhood and kinship in our case.

Eventually, when work was exchanged under a relation of generalised reciprocity with a supernatural subject, God, its economic character was virtually nonexistent; and at the same time, its moral side stood out with utmost intensity; work exchanges no longer bound the members of a particular moral community *as such* but as members of a universal moral community: human society understood as the community of believers and symbolically represented by God. With this, the social construction of work has reached its paramount expression, its most anti-economic dimension, its purest moral form.

Thus far I have been using the concept of moral community as regards different categories of people: farmers, neighbours and kin. But, by rights, the only *moral* community that can be understood as such is the whole of mankind, the community of human beings. Because, as Kant has shown us, morality can be derived only from a universal imperative. Only 'work for God' is a purely moral activity; only religion, therefore, carries the imprint of pure morality. As a matter of fact, were the concept of moral economy to be understood in its deep significance, only the one who is 'working for God' is actually engaged in a moral economy, an economy exempted from any individualistic or material interest, either in the short or long term, an economy that turns out to be the very negation of itself.

'My aim in life is to go to Heaven,' Declan told me on one occasion. 'If at the end of my life I could not go to Heaven I would consider all this a waste of time', he added while he was showing me the work he had been doing on the farm. But times are changing in the west of Ireland. Religiosity is becoming less and less important as the moral fortress of the community. 'God gave to Moses the Ten Commandments,' Declan went on. 'Everybody has to obey them and nobody can get around them, not even the Pope. But now people want to get around the Ten Commandments; the Government is making laws against the Law of God. Going back years that would have never happened.'

Once when I was asking Declan about mutual aid 'in the old days' he made the following observation: 'Aye, everybody was reliable in the farming community. I was telling you about penance: for Lent people would not eat more than one main meal per day, that was the abstinence. People were good Catholics, very good Catholics; they obeyed the Commandments because they knew that if they didn't they would have to pay restitution in the next. They were afraid. But now, there is doubt, there is doubt everywhere, doubt is engrained in everybody's mind, they are not afraid any more … Do you know Joe Greaney up the road, the big farmer? He used to have plenty of machinery a good way back, and he would leave it in the yard unlocked because he knew that nobody would go near it. Ah!, no way you could do that now … ' The demise of religious consciousness has eroded the moral standards of the community, Declan thinks; could that be the reason why informal cooperation is giving way to formal contractual agreements? That is how Declan would look at it. For him, it is the fear of God that makes people comply with their moral duties, and it was the compliance with one's moral duties, we could add, that turned the traditional local economy into a 'moral economy'.

CONCLUDING REMARKS

I would like to stress the underlying motive of our discussion up to this point: to show the ways by which a particular type of *economic* activity, farm work, transforms itself into what appears to be its antithesis, a *social* practice, through the mediation of a specific cultural context. I explained in the Introduction that my intention was to explore the social universe of a farming community of the west of Ireland, trying to answer a simple question: how is work socially construed on a family farm? Our exploration has taken us to different cultural domains, to different dimensions of the local social structure that can all be related to the work of a family farm, either directly or metaphorically. Thus, the social construction of work has become its economic deconstruction. Through this economic deconstruction we have turned the mode of production of western Irish farmers into a concrete social formation.

The opposition between contractual and noncontractual forms of organising work on a farm, or between 'commodity' and 'community' exchanges, has to be understood, first of all, within the framework of the farm productive relations and labour processes. Both types of exchange provide specific normative contexts that can be used alternatively or in combination, depending on the objective necessities of the farm economy, or on the subjective strategies or attitudes of its subjects. But it is important to point out that the farm economy is not immune to those normative contexts; on the contrary, they have important consequences for its constitution as an *economy*.

The 'economy' was our starting point. The economy is an abstract category that tells us very little about social life beyond its own theoretical prejudices. But at the same time, the economy is an intuitive notion very much present not only in our own ideology, that of academic social sciences, but also, and more importantly, in the configuration of the local culture under study. It is present in the harsh materiality of the language of farm work, in the all-pervasive determinism of market forces, which seem to regulate so much of farmers' behaviour. That is why the economy provided such an impeccable point of departure, a springboard that would inevitably lead us to its own dissolution. It has been precisely this process of dissolution of the abstract into the concrete, of the economy into the social, that has constituted my strategy of representation.

There is no clear definition of the social relationships we have been examining in the previous pages, but rather an untidy combination of different notions. We could somehow refer to this combination by underlining three key concepts of our analysis: individualism, morality and sentiment. Neither individualism nor morality nor 'sentimentalism' can be taken as a perfect definition of a concrete economic system such as the one we have been studying. My aim has been to show that elements from those abstract conceptualisations can be found in the mode of production of western Irish farmers. But none of them in itself provides a satisfactory representation of the local economic culture.

Individualism is certainly present in the sphere of market relationships, as it is present in any other market economy. Individualism is not an external ideology imposed by capitalist economy upon a local communitarian ethos. Whatever may be the origin of individualism, external or internal, it cannot be excluded from any accurate representation of rural Irish society. But the sphere of market relationships, where individualist rationality thrives, is not as clear cut as one may think. The sphere of the 'economy' appears definitely embedded in a powerful sociocultural context and, vice versa, that sociocultural context is also pervaded by a certain flavour of economic rationality. As we have repeatedly seen, despite the undeniable economic nature of farm work, it nonetheless seems to possess the strange capacity to participate in other social spheres, those that we would not normally associate with the economy. To understand this transformative capacity of farm work, it is worth recalling a structural homology that was mentioned in an earlier chapter.

We can visualise a farming community as a conglomeration of cross-cutting imaginary circles, each one centred on a different family farm and each one containing all the participants in the labour processes of that particular family farm, arranged according to the social distance that separates them from the farm manager at the centre. In the peripheral regions of those imaginary circles, the economic nature of the farmer's transactions appears with a special intensity. It is very clear in the case of travellers and stock dealers, less so with farm workers and agricultural contractors, and even less with fellow farmers who happen to enter into commodity exchanges with each other. This gradation occurs because those who fall into that periphery do not belong to the farming community as an occupational category, but more importantly, as a moral community. As we come near to the central regions of our imaginary circles, the moral or noneconomic dimension of farm work exchanges stands out with increasing clarity.[1]

Where, we could wonder, does this 'moral effect' come from? What makes the farm economy lose its 'economic' appearance? We could argue that the moral contamination does not stem from the blind obedience of a customary rule, nor from the enigmatic dictates of a 'peasant' rationality, but from the combination of farm work with other spheres of exchange, in such a way that each transaction of this multifarious trade can be 'backed up', so to speak, by the mere cumulative operation of all the rest. In this process we have found particularly relevant two spheres of exchange: kinship and neighbourhood. The overlapping of these two spheres with the sphere of the farm itself enables the development of relations of generalised reciprocity in the farm economy. From this point of view, the individualist ideology incorporated in the commodity form does not seem to have disappeared altogether. It is still present in a kind of long-term perspective, provided by the cumulative effect of those other spheres of exchange.

As we move away from the sphere of contractual transactions, however, the powerful individualistic ethos of the market becomes redefined, if never completely abolished, by the irrationalities of a specific sociocultural context. Kinship and neighbourhood turn the farm economy into a social institution, but they do so because, apart from being spheres of exchange, they appear as moral communities as well. These communities are ruled by a set of rights and obligations that do not have to be explicitly manifest in each particular interaction, since they are taken for

1. '[A clansman] is surrounded by a series of concentric circles each representing the ever widening co-membership spheres to which he belongs. The first circle contains his fellow clansmen, and the next his fellow tribesmen. A measure of kinship distance, then, is the radius of one of these circles. At the periphery, for example, individuals are almost complete strangers, while at the centre they are very closely related. It is only at the periphery that exchange assumes the pure commodity form' (Gregory 1982: 42).

granted. It is this double-sided nature of kinship and neighbourhood, partially moral and partially material, that explains their particular relationship to the farm economy and that enables them, we might speculate, to function as 'emotional containers'.

It has been pointed out that the moral universes of kinship and, to a lesser extent, of neighbourhood act as emotional containers, in such a way that they provide the farm economy with a distinctive character that cannot be easily understood on the basis of a normative/strategical dichotomy. This sphere of the emotional is still a black hole in social analysis. There is little justification for it, especially when we deal with social relations such as kinship that, in the present context, are losing their jural aspect to the advantage of their emotional significance. We are facing a feature of human experience that appears as radically opposed to the individualistic rationality of the market as it is to the holistic morality of religious ideology. This does not mean, on the other hand, that kinship has an exclusively emotional dimension. There is also an important moral aspect both in kinship and in neighbourhood not necessarily linked with the expression of individual sentiments. Still, it seemed to me convenient to stress the irreducibility of this sphere of the emotional and its role in the configuration of a particular type of productive relations.

What I have defined as community in opposition to commodity or market relationships could be visualised as constituted by the following parts. There is an 'emotional' nucleus incarnated in the family unit and a 'moral' periphery wherein kinship links merge with neighbourhood relationships. To a great extent, the closer we come to the family core the more rigid appears the conceptual distinction between kin and neighbours and vice versa. When we arrive at the end of our enquiry into the 'community' side of the commodity/community dichotomy, our initial concern, the farm economy and its labour organisation, has been practically lost, submerged and transfigured into a myriad of social exchanges.

The concept of moral economy is discussed in terms of its antithetic character with both political and 'sentimental' economies. A methodology for the ethnography of economic relationships in western societies seems to lie behind this last concession to abstract reasoning. It is a methodology that might have the virtue of conjuring through description the conceptual quandaries of scientific economists and social theorists. The rational is imposed by the logic of the market, the emotional originates in the intimacy of family relationships and close vicinity, and the moral seems, in this context, almost like a residual category that operates at the periphery of the spheres of kinship and neighbourhood.

They all have a syntagmatic relation with the farm economy; they mix with that economy without being completely absorbed by it.

Neither kinship nor neighbourhood could give rise to the total abrogation of economic rationality because both were part of it; they were syntagmatically related to the farm economy, with their respective spheres of exchange partly blended with the labour organisation of the farm. If we are to find a pure instance of moral economy we have to look for a sphere of exchanges with a paradigmatic relationship to the farm economy. The sphere of exchanges with the supernatural is a sphere that also constitutes a moral community but one much wider than kinship or neighbourhood, since it includes the whole of mankind as a community of believers. The services that circulate within this sphere have no longer a double-sided constitution, as was the case with kinship and neighbourhood; they are purely moral services devoid of any economic significance and they can only be seen as metaphoric 'prestations'. The analysis of religious practices – in particular, penitential practices – concludes in the guise of a phenomenology of exchange what began as a study of economic behaviour. This transformation recalls the transitory and dynamic character of all social formations. We pay a kind of analytical tribute to the holistic moral code once so powerful in the west of Ireland, a moral code that now seems to be on the wane confronted by an unusual alliance of rationality and sentimentalism.

All in all, the result is an economic system that appears very much as the uneasy combination of the rational, the moral and the emotional. Let me restate that it is only the description of a social formation that has motivated the present enquiry. Individualism, morality and sentiment should not be taken as theories of human action in the present context, but simply as clumsy approximations to a rebellious social reality, reverberations of human experience that, it is my hope, might have evoked the intricacies of a particular form of life.

Images and Imagination
A Photographic Appendix

*P*hotographs usually go with ethnographies as illustrations of the written text, if not as merely visual proofs of the author's presence in the field. It is far more uncommon to use photographs as a different type of ethnographic message with its own particular grammar and semantic autonomy, which is precisely what I have attempted to do in the collection that follows. I showed the more than one thousand pictures that I took during my fieldwork in the Three Districts to Domi Mora and Xavier Ribas, two professional photographers and anthropologists, and I asked them to construct their own ethnography with my material. None of them had ever been to Ireland and they did not know much about my research, and yet their 'text' looks strikingly similar to mine. The similarity is weird: it is an interesting way of thinking about the ambiguities of authorship in ethnographic representation. It may be also a way of enlarging its communicative and aesthetic possibilities.

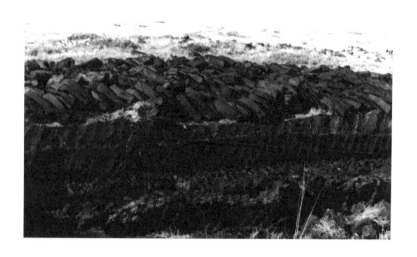

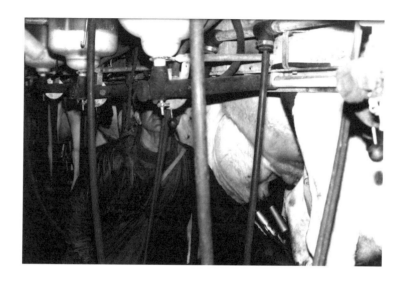

Appendix

BIBLIOGRAPHY

Abrahams, R.G. 'Co–operation on and between Eastern Finnish Family Farms.' In N. Long, ed. *Family and Work in Rural Societies*, London: Tavistock Publications, 1984.

———. *A Place of Their Own. Family Farming in Eastern Finland*. Cambridge: Cambridge University Press, 1991.

Arensberg, C.M. *The Irish Countryman*. London: Macmillan and Co, 1937.

Arensberg, C.M. and S.T. Kimball. *Culture and Community*. New York: Harcourt, Brace and World, Inc., 1965.

———. *Family and Community in Ireland*. 2nd edn. Cambridge, Massachusetts: Harvard University Press, 1968.

Bailey, F.J. 'The Management of Reputations and the Process of Change.' In F.J. Bailey, ed. *Gifts and Poison. The Politics of Reputation*. Oxford: Basil Blackwell, 1971.

Banfield, E.C. *The Moral Basis of a Backward Society*. Glencoe, Illinois: The Free Press, 1958.

Bax, M. 'Patronage Irish Style: Irish Politicians as Brokers.' *Sociologische Gids*, 17 (3) (1970): 179–91.

Bell, J. and M. Watson. *Irish Farming. Implements and Techniques 1750–1900*. Edinburgh: John Donald Publishers Ltd, 1986.

Berkner, L.K. and F.F. Mendels. 'Inheritance Systems, Family Structure and Demographic Patterns in Western Europe, 1700–1900.' In C. Tilly, ed. *Historical Studies of Changing Fertility*. New Jersey: Princeton University Press, 1978.

Bloch, M. 'The Long Term and the Short Term: The Economic and Political Significance of the Morality of Kinship.' In J. Goody, ed. *The Character of Kinship*. Cambridge: Cambridge University Press, 1973.

———. *Prey into Hunter. The Politics of Religious Experience*. Cambridge: Cambridge University Press, 1992.

Bloch, M. and J. Parry. 'Introduction: Money and the Morality of Exchange.' In J. Parry and M. Bloch, eds. *Money and the Morality of Exchange*. Cambridge: Cambridge University Press, 1989.

Bouquet, M. 'Production and Reproduction in South–West England.' *Sociologia Ruralis*, 22 (3/4) (1982): 227–44.

Bibliography

Bouquet, M. *Family, Servants and Visitors. The Farm Household in Nineteenth and Twentieth Century Devon.* Norwich: Geo Books, 1985.

Bouquet, M. and H. De Haan. 'Kinship as an Analytical Category in Rural Sociology: An Introduction.' *Sociologia Ruralis*, 27 (4) (1987): 278–303.

Bourdieu, P. *The Logic of Practice.* Cambridge: Cambridge University Press, 1990.

Brandes, S.H. *Migration, Kinship and Community: Tradition and Transition in a Spanish Village.* Academic Press: New York, 1975.

Breen, R.J. *Up the Airy Mountain and Down the Rushy Glen: Change and Development in an Irish Rural Community.* Cambridge: unpublished Ph.D. thesis, 1981.

———. 'Farm Servanthood in Ireland, 1900–40.' *The Economic History Review*, XXXVI (1) (1983): 87–102.

———. 'Population Trends in Late Nineteenth Century and Early Twentieth Century in Ireland: A local Study.' *The Economic and Social Review*, 15 (2) (1984): 95–108.

Breen, R., D.F. Hannan, D.B. Rottman and C.T. Whelan. *Understanding Contemporary Ireland.* Dublin: Gill and Macmillan, 1990.

Brody, H. *Inishkillane. Change and Decline in the West of Ireland.* London: Allen Lane The Penguin Press, 1973.

Brown, T. *Ireland. A Social and Cultural History 1922–1985.* London: Fontana Press, 1985.

Buttel, F.H. and H. Newby. 'Toward a Critical Rural Sociology.' In F.H. Buttel and H. Newby, eds. *The Rural Sociology of Advanced Societies.* London: Croom Helm, 1980.

Cambrensis, G. (12th century) *Topography of Ireland.* Dundalk: Dundalgan Press, 1951.

Campbell, J.K. *Honour, Family, and Patronage. A Study of Institutions and Moral Values in a Greek Mountain Community.* Oxford: Oxford University Press, 1964.

Cheal, D. *The Gift Economy.* London: Routledge, 1988.

Clark, S. *Social Origins of the Irish Land War.* New Jersey: Princeton University Press, 1979.

Codd, N. 'Reputation and Social Structure in a Spanish Pyrenean Village.' In F.J. Bailey, ed. *Gifts and Poison. The Politics of Reputation.* Oxford: Basil Blackwell, 1971.

Cohen, A.P. *Whalsay. Symbol, Segment and Boundary in a Shetland Island Community.* Manchester: Manchester University Press, 1987.

Cole, J.W. and E.R. Wolf. *The Hidden Frontier. Encology and Ethnicity in an Alpine Valley.* New York and London: Academic Press, 1974.

Commins, P. *Farm Structures and Pluriactivity. Research Programme on Rural Change in Europe. First Pannel of Interviews 1989 Corresponding to Ireland. Summary Report.* Dublin: Rural Economy Research Center, Teagasc (Agriculture and Food Development Authority), unpublished manuscript, 1990.

Connacht Tribune, 13 July 1990.

Connell, K.H. *Irish Peasant Society.* Oxford: Clarendon Press, 1968.

Cuddy, M. and C. Curtin. 'Commercialisation in West of Ireland Agriculture in the 1890s.' *The Economic and Social Review*, 14 (3) (1983): 173–84.

Curtin, C. 'The Peasant Family farm and Comoditization in the West of Ireland.' In N. Long, J.D. Van Der Ploeg, C. Curtin and L. Box. *The Commoditization Debate: Labour Process, Strategy and Social Network.* Wageningen: Agricultural University Wageningen, 1986.

Curtin, C. and A. Varley. 'Collusion Practices in a West of Ireland Livestock Mart.' *Ethnology*, XXI (4) (1982): 349–57.

———. 'Children and Childhood in Rural Ireland: A Consideration of the Ethnographic Literature.' In C. Curtin, M. Kelly and L. O'Dowd, eds. *Culture and Ideology in Ireland*. Galway: Galway University Press, 1984.

———. 'Cooperation and Rural Development in the West of Ireland.' *Eire-Ireland. A Journal of Irish Studies*, (XXIV) (1989): 104–19.

Danaher, K. *The Year in Ireland. Irish Calendar Customs*. Cork and Dublin: The Mercier Press, 1972.

Davies, J.E. 'Capitalist Agricultural Development and the Exploitation of the Propertied Labourer.' In F.H. Buttel and H. Newby, eds. *The Rural Sociology of Advanced Societies. Critical Perspectives*. London: Croom Helm, 1980.

Dilley, R. 'Contesting Markets: A General Introduction to Market Ideology, Imagery and Discourse.' In R. Dilley, ed. *Contesting Markets. Analysis of Ideology, Discourse and Practice*. Edinburgh: Edinburgh University Press, 1992.

Donham, D.L. 'Beyond the Domestic Mode of Production', *Man* (N.S.) 16 (1981): 516–41.

Dubisch, J. 'Introduction.' In J. Dubisch, ed. *Gender and Power in Rural Greece*. Princeton: Princeton University Press, 1986.

Duggan, C. 'Farming Women or Farmers' Wives? Women in the Farming Press.' In C. Curtin, P.O. Jackson and B. Coonor, eds. *Gender in Irish Society*. Galway: Galway University Press, 1987.

Dumont, L. *From Mandeville to Marx. The Genesis and Triumph of Economic Ideology*. Chicago and London: The University of Chicago Press, 1977.

Emmett, I. *A North Wales Village. A Social Anthropological Study*. London: Routledge and Kegan Paul, 1964.

Erasmus, C.J. 'Culture Structure and Process: The Occurrence and Disappearance of Reciprocal Farm Labor.' *Southwestern Journal of Anthropology*, 12 (4) (1956): 444–69.

Evans, E.E. *Irish Heritage. The Landscape, the People and their Work*. Dundalk: Dundalk Press, 1942.

———. *Irish Folk Ways*. London: Routledge and Kegan Paul, 1957.

Evans-Pritchard, E.E. *The Nuer*. Oxford: Oxford University Press, 1940.

Evers, H.D. and H. Schrader, eds. *The Moral Economy of Trade. Ethnicity and Developing Markets*. London: Routledge, 1994.

Fitzpatrick, D. 'Irish Farming Families before the First World War.' *Comparative Studies in Society and History*, 25 (1983): 339–74.

Fortes, M. *Kinship and the Social Order*. London: Routledge and Kegan Paul, 1969.

Foster, G.M. 'The Dyadic Contract: A Model for the Social Structure of a Mexican Peasant Village.' *American Anthropologist*, 63 (1961): 1173–92.

———. 'The Dyadic Contract in Tzintzuntzan, II: Patron–client Relationship.' *American Anthropologist*, 65 (6) (1963): 1280–94.

Foster, R.F. *Modern Ireland 1600–1972*. London: Alan Lane the Penguin Press, 1988.

Fox, R. *Kinship and Marriage. An Anthropological Perspective*. Cambridge: Cambridge University Press, 1967.

———. *The Tory Islanders. A People of the Celtic Fringe*. Cambridge: Cambridge University Press, 1978.

Freeman, S.T. *Neighbors. The Social Contract in a Castilian Hamlet.* Chicago: The University of Chicago Press, 1970.

Freeman, T.W. *Ireland. A General and Regional Geography.* London: Methuen and Co., Ltd., 1969.

Friedl, E. 'The Position of Women: Appearance and Reality.' In J. Dubisch, ed. *Gender and Power in Rural Greece.* Reprint. Princeton: Princeton University Press, 1986.

Gell, A. 'Intertribal Commodity Barter and Reproductive Gift–Exchange in Old Melanesia.' In C. Humphrey and S. Hugh-Jones, eds. *Barter, Exchange and Value. An Anthropological Approach.* Cambridge: Cambridge University Press, 1992.

Gibbon, P. 'Arensberg and Kimball Revisited.' *Economy and Society,* 2 (4) (1973): 479–98.

Gibbon, P. and C. Curtin. 'The Stem Family in Ireland.' *Comparative Studies in Society and History,* 20 (1978): 429–53.

———. 'Irish Farm Families. Facts and Fantasies.' *Comparative Studies in Society and History,* 25 (1983): 375–80.

Giddens, A. *The Constitution of Society.* Cambridge: Polity Press, 1984.

Gilmore, D.D. 'Men and Women in Southern Spain: "Domestic Power" Revisited.' *American Anthropologist,* 92 (4) (1990): 953–70.

Glassie, H. *Passing the Time. Folklore and History of an Ulster Community.* Dublin: The O'Brien Press Ltd, 1982.

Gmelch, G. *The Irish Tinkers. The Urbanization of an Itinerant People.* California: Cummings Publishing Company, Inc., 1977.

Goody, J. *Production and Reproduction.* Cambridge: Cambridge University Press, 1976.

———. *The Development of the Family and Marriage in Europe.* Cambridge: Cambridge University Press, 1983.

Gouldner, A.W. 'The Norm of Reciprocity: A Preliminary Statement.' *American Sociological Review,* 25 (2) (1960): 161–78.

Gray, J.N. 'Lamb Auctions on the Borders.' *European Journal of Sociology,* 25 (1984): 54–82.

Gregory, C.A. *Gifts and Commodities.* London: Academic Press, 1982.

Gudeman, S. *Economics as Culture. Models and Metaphors of Livelihood.* London: Routledge and Kegan Paul, 1986.

Gudeman, S. and A. Rivera. *Conversations in Colombia. The Domestic Economy in Life and Text.* Cambridge: Cambridge University Press, 1990.

Habakkuk, H.J. 'Family Structure and Economic Change in Nineteenth–Century Europe.' *The Journal of Economic History,* XV (1) (1955): 1–12.

Hannan, D.F. 'Kinship, Neighbourhood and Social Change in Irish Rural Communities.' *The Economic and Social Review,* 3 (2) (1972): 163–88.

———. *Displacement and Development: Class, Kinship and Social Change in Irish Rural Communities.* Dublin: The Economic and Social Research Institute, 1979.

Hannan, D.F. and L.A. Katsiaouni. *Traditional families?: From Culturally Prescribed to Negotiated Roles in Farm Families.* Dublin: The Economic and Social Research Institute, 1977.

Hanssen, B. 'Household, Class, and Integration Process in a Scandinavian Village over 300 Years.' *Ethnologia Europæa,* XI (1) (1979/80): 76–118.

Harris, L. 'Class Community and Sexual Divisions in North Mayo.' In C. Curtin, M. Kelly and L. O'Dowd, eds. *Culture and Ideology in Ireland*. Galway: Galway University Press, 1984.

Harris, R. *Prejudice and Tolerance in Ulster*. Manchester: Manchester University Press, 1972.

———. 'Theory and Evidence. The "Irish Stem Family" and Field Data.' *Man* (N.S.), 23 (3) (1988): 417–34.

Hart, K. 'On Commoditization.' In E.N. Goody, ed. *From Craft to Industry. The Ethnography of Proto–industrial Cloth Production*. Cambridge: Cambridge University Press, 1982.

———. 'Heads or Tails? Two Sides of the Coin.' *Man* (N.S.), 21 (4) (1986): 637–56.

Hubert, H. and M. Mauss. *Sacrifice. Its Nature and Functions*. Chicago: The University of Chicago Press, 1964.

Humphrey, C. and S. Hugh-Jones, eds. *Barter, Exchange and Value. An Anthropological Approach*. Cambridge: Cambridge University Press, 1992.

Humphreys, A.J. *New Dubliners. Urbanization and the Irish Family*. London: Routledge and Kegan Paul, 1966.

Hutchinson, B. 'On the Study of Non–Economic Factors in Irish Economic Development.' *Economic and Social Review*, 1 (4) (1970): 509–527.

Inglis, T. *Moral Monopoly. The Catholic Church in Modern Irish Society*. Dublin: Gill and Macmillan Ltd, 1987.

Irish Independent, 24 April 1990.

Iturra, R. 'Strategies in Social Recruitment: A Case of Mutual Help in Rural Galicia.' *The Queen's University Papers in Social Anthropology*, 2 (1977): 75–93.

Kane, E. 'Man and Kin in Donegal: A Study of Kinship Functions in a Rural Irish and Irish–American Community.' *Ethnology*, VII (3) (1968): 245–58.

———. 'The Changing Role of the Family in a Rural Irish Community.' *Journal of Comparative Family Studies*, 10 (1979): 141–62.

Kennedy, R.E. *The Irish. Emigration, Marriage, and Fertility*. Berkley and Los Angeles: University of California Press, 1973.

Kopytoff, I. 'The Cultural Biography of Things: Commoditization as Process.' In A. Appadurai, ed. *The Social Life of Things. Commodities in Cultural Perspective*. Cambridge: Cambridge University Press, 1986.

Laslett, P. 'The Family as a Knot of Individual Interests.' In R. McC. Netting, R.R. Wilk and E.J. Arnould, eds. *Houselhods. Comparative and Historical Studies of the Domestic Group*. Berkeley: University of California Press, 1984.

Leeuwis, C. *Marginalization Misunderstood. Different Patterns of Farm Development in the West of Ireland*. Wageningen: Agricultural University, 1986.

Leyton, E. 'The One Blood. Kinship and Class in an Irish Village.' *Newfoundland Social and Economic Studies*, 15 (1975).

Long, N. 'The Social Reproduction of Petty Commodity Enterprise in Central Peru.' In N. Long, J.D. Van Der Ploeg, C. Curtin and L. Box. *The Commoditization Debate: Labour Process, Strategy and Social Network*. Wageningen: Agricultural University Wageningen, 1986.

Macfarlane, A. *Marriage and Love in England. Modes of Reproduction 1300–1840*. Oxford: Basil Blackwell, 1986.

———. *The Culture of Capitalism*. Oxford: Basil Blackwell, 1987.

Maine, H.S. *Ancient Law*. Reprint. Tucson: The University of Arizona Press, 1986.

Malinowski, B. *Argonauts of Western Pacific*. London and New York: Routledge and Kegan Paul, 1922.

Marx, K. *Capital*. Harmondsworth: Penguin Books, 1976.

Mauss, M. *The Gift*. London: Routledge, 1990.

McAleese, D. 'Political Independence, Economic Growth and the Role of Economic Policy.' In P.J. Drudy, ed. *Ireland: Land, Politics and People*. Cambridge: Cambridge University Press, 1982.

McGahern, J. *The Barracks*. London: Faber and Faber, 1963.

———. *Amongst Women*. London: Faber and Faber, 1990.

McNabb, P. 'Social Structure.' In J. Newmann, ed. *The Limerick Survey 1958–1964*. Tipperary: Muintir Na Tire Publications, 1964.

Medick, H. and D.W. Sabean. 'Interest and Emotion in Family and Kinship Studies: A Critique of Social History and Anthropology.' In H. Medick and D.W. Sabean, eds. *Interest and Emotion. Essays on the Study of Family and Kinship* Cambridge: Cambridge University Press, 1984.

Mendras, H. *The Vanishing Peasant. Innovation and Change in French Agriculture*. Cambridge, Massachusetts: The MIT Press, 1970.

Messenger, J.C. *Inis Beag. Isle of Ireland*. New York: Holt, Rinehart and Winston, 1969.

Mewett, P.G. 'Associational Categories and the Social Location of Relationships in a Lewis Crofting Community.' In A. Cohen, ed. *Belonging. Identity and Social Organisation in British Rural Cultures*. Manchester: Manchester University Press, 1982.

National Farm Survey: Provisional Estimates. Dublin: Agricultural and Food Development Authority, Rural Economy, 1989.

Newby, H. *The Deferential Worker. A Study of Farm Workers in East Anglia*. London: Penguin Books, 1977.

———. *Green and Pleasant Land? Social Change in Rural England*. London: Wildwood House, 1979.

Ó Cinneide, M.S. and M.E. Cawley. *Development of Agriculture in the West of Ireland 1970–1980*. Blackrock: Council for Development in Agriculture, 1983.

O'Dowd, A. *Meitheal. A Study of Co–operative Labour in Rural Ireland*. Dublin: Leinster Leader Ltd., 1981.

Ó Fiaich, T. 'The Language and Political History.' In B. O Cuiv, ed. *A View of the Irish Language*. Dublin: Stationary Office, 1969.

O'Neill, B.J. *Social Inequality in a Portuguese Hamlet. Land, Late marriage, and Bastardy, 1870–1978*. Cambridge: Cambridge University Press, 1987.

O'Neill, K. *Family and Farm in Pre–Famine Ireland*. Madison Wisconsin: University of Wisconsin Press, 1984.

Ott, S. *The Circle of Mountains. A Basque Shepherding Community*. Oxford: Clarendon Press, 1981.

Petty, W. *The Political Anatomy of Ireland*. Reprint. Dublin: Irish University Press, 1979.

Pina-Cabral, J. *Sons of Adam, Daughters of Eve. The Peasant Worldview of the Alto Minho*. Oxford: Clarendon Press, 1986.

Pitt-Rivers, J.A. *The People of the Sierra*. 2nd edn. Chicago: The University of Chicago Press, 1971.

———. 'The Kith and the Kin.' In J. Goody, ed. *The Character of Kinship*. Cambridge: Cambridge University Press, 1973.

Popkin, S.L. *The Rational Peasant. The Political Economy of Rural Society in Vietnam.* Berkeley and Los Angeles: University of California Press, 1979.

Rees, A.D. *Life in a Welsh Countryside. A Social Study of Llanfihangel yng Ngwynfa.* Cardiff: University of Wales Press, 1950.

Rogers, S.C. 'Female Forms of Power and the Myth of Male Dominance: A Model of Female/Male Interaction in Peasant Society.' *American Ethnologist*, 2 (4) (1975): 727–56.

———. 'Gender in Southwestern France: The Myth of Male Dominance Revisited.' *Anthropology*, 9 (1985): 65–86.

———. *Shaping Modern Times in Rural France.* Princeton: Princeton University Press, 1991.

Russell, J.C. *In the Shadow of Saints: Aspects of Family and Religion in a Rural Irish Gaeltacht Community.* University of California: unpublished Ph.D. dissertation, 1979.

Sahlins, M. *Stone Age Economics.* London and New York: Routledge, 1972.

Salazar, C. 'The Inmates: Countrywomen in the West of Ireland.' Belfast: unpublished paper presented at the 1st 1991 Conference of the Anthropological Association of Ireland.

———. 'On Blood and Its Alternatives. An Irish History.' Oslo: unpublished paper presented at the 3rd EASA Conference, 1994.

Scheper-Hughes, N. *Saints, Scholars, and Schizophrenics. Mental Illness in Rural Ireland.* Berkeley: University of California Press, 1979.

Schneider, D.M. *American Kinship: A Cultural Account.* Englewood Cliffs, New Jersey: Prentice–Hall, Inc., 1968.

Scott, J.C. *The Moral Economy of the Peasant. Rebellion and Subsistence in Southeast Asia.* New Haven and London: Yale University Press, 1976.

Segalen, M. *Historical Anthropology of the Family.* Cambridge: Cambridge University Press, 1986.

Sheehy, S.J and R. O'Connor. *Economics of Irish Agriculture.* Dublin: Institute of Public Administration, 1985.

Shortall, S. 'The Dearth of Data on Irish Farm Wives: A Critical Review of the Literature.' *The Economic and Social Review*, 22 (4) (1991): 311–32.

Silverman, S.F. 'Agricultural Organization, Social Structure, and Values in Italy: Amoral Familism Reconsidered.' *American Anthropologist*, 70 (1968): 1–20.

Strathern, M. 'Kinship and Economy: Constitutive Orders of a Provisional Kind.' *American Ethnologist*, 12 (2) (1985): 191–209.

Symes, D.G. 'Farm Household and Farm Performance: A Study of Twentieth Century Changes in Ballyferriter, Southwest Ireland.' *Ethnology*, XI (1) (1972): 25–38.

Synge, J.M. *The Aran Islands.* Oxford: Oxford University Press, 1979.

———. *The Playboy of the Western World.* London: Methuen, 1983.

Taylor, L.J. 'Colonialism and Community Structure in Western Ireland.' *Ethnohistory*, 27 (1980): 169–81.

Thomas, W.I. and F. Znaniecki. *The Polish Peasant in Europe and America.* Abridged edn. Urbana and Chicago: University of Illinois Press, 1984.

Thompson, E.P. 'The Moral Economy of the English Crowd in the Eighteenth Century.' *Past and Present*, 50 (1971): 76–136.

Thompson, P. *The Nature of Work. An Introduction to Debates on the Labour Process.* London: Macmillan Press Ltd., 1983.

Tönnies, F. *Community and Association.* London: Routledge and Kegan Paul, 1974.

Tuam Herald, 25 May 1991.

Turner, V. and E. Turner. *Image and Pilgrimage in Christian Culture. Anthropological Perspectives.* Oxford: Basil Blackwell, 1978.

Van Der Ploeg, J.D. 'The Agricultural Labour Process and Commoditization.' In N. Long, J.D. Van Der Ploeg, C. Curtin and L. Box. *The Commoditization Debate: Labour Process, Strategy and Social Network.* Wageningen: Agricultural University Wageningen, 1986.

Varley, A. '"The Stem Family in Ireland" Reconsidered.' *Comparative Studies in Society and History,* 25 (1983): 381–92.

Wall, M. 'The Decline of the Irish Language.' In B. O Cuiv, ed. *A view of the Irish language.* Dublin: Stationary Office, 1969.

Whatmore, S. 'Life Cycle or Patriarchy? Gender Divisions in Family Farming.' *Journal of Rural Studies,* 7 (1/2) (1991): 71–76.

Wickham, J. 'Industrialisation, Work and Unemployment': In P. Clancy, D. Sheelagh, K. Lynch and L. O'Dowd, eds. *Ireland: a Sociological Profile.* Dublin: Institute of Public Administration in association with The Sociological Association of Ireland, 1986.

Williams, W.M. *The Sociology of an English Village. Gosforth.* London: Routledge and Kegan Paul Ltd., 1956.

Williams, W.M. *A West Country Village. Ashworthy. Family, Kinship and Land.* London: Routledge and Kegan Paul Ltd., 1963.

Wilson, T.M. 'From Clare to the Common Market: Perspectives in Irish Ethnography.' *Anthropological Quarterly,* 57 (1) (1984): 1–15.

Young, M. and P. Willmott. *Family and Kinship in East London.* Revised edn. Harmondsworth: Penguin Books, 1986.

175

Index

embedded, 31, 63n, 146, 150
house, 29
intuitive notion, 25, 150
moral, 125ff, 132, 138, 147, 148, 152, 153
natural, 26
political, 5, 126
sentimental, 138, 152
world, 24, 33, 34, 126
endogamy of farmers, 52, 129; *see also* local exogamy, marriage
England, 21n, 24, 46, 47, 68, 104n, 109, 123
ethnic identity, 83
ethnographic research, *see* participant observation
Europe, European Community, 1, 15, 24, 28, 33, 48, 80, 83, 89n, 101, 102
Evans-Pritchard, E.E., 14
externalisation, 29

fairs
livestock, 34ff, 115
of farm labourers, 48ff
family size, 104; *see also* fertility
Famine, 46, 53n, 95
fasting and abstinence, 140, 141, 145, 147
feminist anthropology, 101–2
fertility, 103–5
fieldwork ethics, 12
Fortes, M., 130, 131n
fosterage and adoption, 108, 110, 124, 133, 135
funerals, 123, 141

Gaeltacht, 45, 47, 48, 50, 95; *see also* Irish language
generalised reciprocity, 12, 62, 69, 70n, 72, 73, 84, 85, 90, 126, 127, 128, 130, 142, 144, 146, 147, 151; *see also* cooperative attitudes and work, gift exchanges, informal exchanges, non-commodity exchanges, noncontractual relationships, work exchanges
Giddens, A., 10
gift exchanges, 5, 63n, 73, 82n, 89n, 90, 109, 127, 136n, 143n; *see also* generalised reciprocity, noncommodity exchanges
Goody, J., 108
gossip, 118, 119, 120, 121ff

humanistic ethnography, 10

indebtedness
with fodder suppliers, 28
with God, 144ff

individualism, individualisation, 76, 77, 78, 79, 81, 126, 127, 136, 138, 147, 150, 151, 152, 153
methodological, 127, 132
industrialisation, 24, 28, 48
inequalities in reciprocal exchanges, 87, 90–91; *see also* machinery loans
informal exchanges, cooperation, transactions, 13, 61, 72, 73, 74, 84, 85, 92, 126, 127, 148; *see also* cooperative attitudes and work, coor, generalised reciprocity, noncommodity exchanges, noncontractual relationships, work exchanges
inheritance, 54, 94, 95, 102, 129, 136
integration, 28
intervention, 33

labour process in industry, 56
land
holding size, 4, 74
husbandry, 14, 17ff
ownership, 87, 114
landlords, 8, 17, 39n
landscape, 7, 13, 17ff, 48
language
cryptic, 36
Irish, 45–50; *see also* Gaeltacht
of farm work, 2, 14, 85, 86, 90, 116, 150
Laslett, P., 96n
local exogamy, 100, 129; *see also* endogamy of farmers, marriage
luck money, 60, 65

machinery loans, 61, 75, 85, 86, 87, 91, 92, 148; *see also* inequalities in reciprocal exchanges
Maine, H.S., 72, 73
Malinowski, B., 72n, 89n
market and commodity exchanges, 5, 15, 26, 27, 33, 34, 38, 39, 40n, 62n, 65, 67, 80, 81, 92, 94, 96, 126, 127n, 132, 150, 152; *see also* commoditisation, capitalism, capitalist and commoditised economy
marriage, 97, 98, 100, 109, 110, 130n, 135, 136; *see also* endogamy of farmers, local exogamy
mart, 35ff, 50, 59, 72, 80; *see also* cooperative
Marx, K., 40, 91
Mauss, M., 73, 143
mechanisation, 17, 18, 20, 21, 44, 50, 53n, 56, 79, 96, 104, 105
misrecognition of women's farm work, 31, 102